Flowers on the Balcony

20 Calls to Action to Transform Your Life

ISBN-13: 978-1-962185-04-2

Text Copyright © 2023 Marcos H. N. Rossi

Published by Underline Publishing LLC
www.underlinepublishing.com

All rights reserved.

No part of this publication may be reproduced, distributed or transmitted in any form or by any means, or stored in a database or retrieval system, without the prior written permission of the publisher. The only exception is by a reviewer, who may quote short excerpts in a review.

This is a work of fiction. Names, characters, business, events and incidents are the products of the author's imagination. Any resemblance to actual persons, living or dead, or actual events is purely coincidental.

Acknowledgments

First of all, I would like to thank my wife Vânia. Without her constant encouragement, patience, and dedication to revise and critique each essay prior to its publication, this book simply would not exist. She is almost a co-author.

Second, I must thank all the readers of the blog that originated the book, who not only took the time to read, but also to provide feedback through comments, suggestions, and words of encouragement. Without your support, I would never have achieved the realization of this dream.

Then, comes a very special "thank you" to all the readers of my three books published in the last ten years. You are my fuel to keep going. My deepest gratitude for every phone call, email, text message, and comment on my social media and the positive reviews posted on online retailers.

Finally, I would like to express my eternal gratitude to Nereide Santa Rosa. Without her unrestricted support, the dream of publishing this revised and improved version of my first literary work simply would not be possible.

Other books by
Marcos H. N. Rossi:

Os Caminhos do Amor em Bread & Joy
Flores na Varanda
A Mais Bela Travessia

Receive information about
new releases by this author by
subscribing to our newsletter:

Preface to the 10th Anniversary Commemorative Edition

At the end of 2012, possibly October or November, I experienced one of the most rewarding moments of my life. I received at home a long-awaited package that carried a unit of my first "literary son" (it is customary for publishers to send a non-commercial copy for the author's approval).

I ran into the house and, taking advantage of the fact that I was alone, savored that moment with all the intensity that it deserved.

As I opened the package, emotions took over me, and tears ran down my face. After twenty-odd months of work, publishing one essay a month in a blog, and going through the whole process of transforming the content to the format required by the publisher, the first unit was in my hands.

I embraced it fondly and remembered every step I took to get there. I had fulfilled a dream that, two years earlier, seemed just surreal.

However, after a more thorough review, to my frustration, I found some errors and had to postpone the final publication for a couple of months.

That leads us to January 26, 2013, when I gathered friends and family in an event hall of a hotel in Doral, Florida, and together we celebrated the official launch of "Flowers on the Balcony."

Ten years passed since, and what was supposed to be just a "literary adventure" shared only with my inner circle, took on unimaginable proportions. "Flowers" reached a huge audience, and its success led to its two literary "brothers":

The Paths of Love in Bread & Joy, and The Most Beautiful Crossing (for now, only available in Portuguese).

Thanks to Underline Publishing, I was able to unify my work under just one publisher, globally.

As we began the work of republishing "Flowers," it became evident that ten years had been enough to render some habits and expressions antiquated, if not obsolete. Thus, we took the opportunity to revise the content and make it not only more up to date, but less vulnerable to the passing of time. After all, the essence of the twenty essays is timeless, since placing our flowers on the balcony will never cease to be a metaphor that will have its place, yesterday, today, and always.

Happy tenth anniversary, "Flowers on the Balcony." May you continue to touch hearts for many years to come.

Revised Original Preface

In the fall of 2010, my life went through some changes that were fundamental for this book to become a reality. Being transferred to a new area at work would lead me to meet new people and new assignments. However, it would also lead me to new ideas, new books, and new personal projects, including starting to write.

I felt this desire of writing for many years. The first drafts came out in my late teens, when I was 18 or 19. All I needed was to put my head down on the pillow for my mind to begin to wander, creating the most beautiful poems and essays that never found pen and paper. Until one night I got up and wrote my first text, entitled "Pillow Poet," which ended precisely saying that one day, these phrases and ideas would leave my mind and find a place to materialize. Other essays came later, and I know I have them in some drawer, but that is all they ever came to be, manuscripts kept in a drawer.

With the work obligations that followed, the desire to write was gradually forgotten and was locked up for decades. However, after a long time, this desire to express myself came back strong. Some "gems" came out and were published on a family photo blog, receiving much praise from relatives and friends.

Which brings us back to the fall of 2010, that brought along a moment of personal transformation. New influences made me rethink my life and the best use of my free time. However, one concept in particular was especially useful to me. If we want to get different results, we need to do something different, run the extra mile, do what others don't do, like waking up at 5 a.m. to start the day.

So, I started nurturing the idea of waking up early to write. But write about what? And how would I publish what I write? That's when I heard an inner voice saying that I should write short essays about values and things that could motivate and inspire other people, so that they too could seek their personal transformation. The idea of creating a blog as a means to publish came next. And then, the necessary conditions were fulfilled for the creation of Flowers on the Balcony. I had found the time, the purpose, the media, and the desire.

I created the blog and published the first essay (which gave name to the blog and later to this book) in January 2011, and since then, my followers and I have shared moments of joy, self-discovery and, of course, transformation. We talked about doing good deeds, parenthood, about making a difference, love, forgiveness, relationships, music, mental and spiritual health, midlife crisis, creativity, self-leadership, living life to the fullest and much more.

It was almost two years of adventure and companionship, waking up early to share my thoughts. All twenty essays were written twice, first in Portuguese and then in English. The result fills me with joy and can be read in sequence or randomly, as each essay addresses a different topic.

But they all have one thing in common. All twenty essays have a call to action that, if answered, are sure to bring transformation. They all end with some questioning and suggestions for behavioral changes that aim to improve the lives and the world of readers. So, I decided to make it easier and had them listed at the end.

Today, the blog is no longer online, since the content is here in this book. In gathering the twenty essays here, I became aware of certain repetitions, such as three quotes from Gandhi and two from the film Forrest Gump. I decided to keep them, as they are perfect openings for their essays.

I wish you a joyful reading and that it serves as motivation for your personal transformation. As you reach the end, I hope your balcony (which for those who have not yet understood the metaphor, is your own life) will be renewed and full of flowers.

Contents

Flowers on the Balcony 13
Parenting In Perspective 19
Making the Difference 25
My Musical Rollercoaster 31
The Love Proposition 37
The "Lucca-Peto" Balance 45
Doing Good Deeds Because We Must 51
Cultivating The Garden of The Mind 59
Our Daily Agnus Dei 65
The Piece of Paper that Changed My Life 73
The Race That Is Worth Running 81
The Midlife Opportunity 89
About Passion and Detachment 95
The Power of Perseverance 103
Shine and Let Shine 103
Taking Good Care of Our Love Triangles 111
Don't Become a Garbage Truck 119
The Da Vinci Complex 125
Prisoners of the Cost-Benefit Analysis 131
Be the Maestro of Your Life 139
Living Life to the Fullest as if We Were Going to Die 145
The Twenty Calls to Action 153

FLOWERS ON THE BALCONY

"You must be the change you want to see in the world"
Gandhi

I cannot tell you precisely where or when I heard this story for the first time, but I believe it was in some movie, that I hope one day will cross my path again, so I may watch it once more. That is how it is, many times in life. Good things cross our paths, touch our hearts in one way or another, but we don't let them in. We don't digest them. We don't register them. We don't take note of the license plate. And if our day to day doesn't bring us a practical situation where such learning may be applied, that little piece of wisdom is lost, and there goes another gem, that was given to us by life as a gift.

I think one of the ambitions of this book is to register these events that, believe it or not, happen every day. They happen when we watch a good movie, read a good book, listen to a great song, watch a good TV show, or even in practical situations of our day to day when we interact with other people. These gems are given to us frequently.

It is our duty to recognize them, keep them safe and use them as such.

Since I did not take notes on this gem at the right moment, what follows is part memory, part fiction, but I hope it will reach its objective.

Our story is about a lady named Lilly who, in one of these drastic shifts that life brings every now and then, had to move to a smaller apartment, located in a less privileged neighborhood. The building was old, the place was quite small and needed some heavy cleaning.

However, what got Lilly's attention the most was that the living room had a small balcony that led to the back of the building, where one could see the back of other buildings of the same architecture, with many other balconies. The view was sad. Everything was grey and lifeless.

Lilly was a strong woman, with a positive attitude about life and people. Nothing would easily bring her energy and inner light down.

She cleaned the apartment, decorated it simply but harmonically, and made her new place, although humble, a very pleasant home.

But that balcony would still bother her. Every time she would go out there, she would feel a bit depressed. Until one day she got tired of such a situation and decided to change it.

With some small savings she still had, she went out to a flower shop nearby and bought a variety of flowerpots with many types and colors and decorated her balcony with devotion. When she was done, she went down to the alley and looked up, to contemplate her work of art (after all, that is what it was) full of pride. That balcony would jump into one's eyes. In a lifeless grey alley, where every balcony looked the same, hers would stand out. It felt like an oasis in the desert. Oh, how beautiful that balcony was.

Flowers on the Balcony

While she was there, lost in her moments of contemplation, Lilly did not notice the approach of two other ladies. With their mouths dropped and eyes locked on the new balcony, they came and positioned side by side with Lilly.

Lilly suddenly realized she was not alone and quickly decided to introduce herself to the new neighbors. What happened next was something that Lilly was not expecting. The neighbor to the right immediately started to criticize her for the waste of money, for being so vain and for trying to diminish the neighbors with her egotistic attitude. She said that if Lilly wasn't happy with her new neighborhood the way it was, she should look for another one. Then she turned her back on Lilly and, whining, went back to her routine. However, the other neighbor was amazed with the change that Lilly's balcony brought to that grey alley and said it would be wonderful if she could do the same. Lilly invited her in for a cup of tea and promised to help her new friend. She shared some of her new flowers with her, and together, little by little when some change became available, they decorated both balconies. They brought new colors to that alley that looked no longer as grey.

A few weeks later, another neighbor came to them wanting to know how they decorated their balconies so beautifully. Soon, a third decorated balcony showed up. And soon, another one appeared. And then another. And another. In a matter of months that sad and lifeless alley was full of colors. Whoever passed by would stop to admire the widest variety of flowers, and in the air, one could notice the most pleasant aromas.

The neighbor that once had criticized Lilly now had one of the few balconies without flowers. It stood out lifelessly amongst so much color and beauty that emanated from the other balconies.

The neighbors that would rarely talk to each other in the past, now would gather there in the alley at the end of each afternoon to admire their balconies, have a cup of tea, talk about life, exchange ideas, and every now and then, would promote family gatherings when they would share what they had, bringing joy to each other.

Lilly could never predict that her simple act of putting flowers on her balcony, would have that kind of impact on her neighborhood, and would change for the better the life of people around her in such dramatic way, and of course, her own.

Now stop for a moment and think about this story and how it resembles our lives. Let it sink in and wander around your head a little. Try to remember the times in your life when something similar happened to you.

How many times have we played one of these different roles? How many times might we have played the role of that negative neighbor and criticized our own neighbor, a friend, a sibling, a parent, a son/daughter, a coworker, a lover, for simply acting or thinking differently, or for trying to put their flowers on the balcony? How often do we actually act as the other neighbor that showed sympathy over the new and let change and a new attitude to come and impact her life? For how many times have we tried to do what Lilly did, putting our flowers on the balcony, but cowardly ran out and brought every pot of flowers in, at the first criticism we received? And how many times have we looked at people who wanted to follow our good example as full of envy, just willing to take a ride in our successes, shutting the door for a new relationship to grow, wasting the opportunity to make a new friend and a new ally?

In a given moment of my professional life, I had to face a grey alley. I was leading a department that, although small, was critical for the company, in an environment of extreme pressure, where people would be blaming each other all the time for what went wrong and would frequently argue and be disrespectful to one another. There were moments when the work environment would be close to unbearable and would make everybody stressed and unhappy.

Tired of that reality, one day I gathered the whole team in my office and told them that, if we were all unhappy with such a work environment, we should take action to change it. I used the metaphor of the flowers on the balcony and proposed that from that moment on, every coworker would be served with a smile. That we would use expressions such as "please," "thank you very much," "how can I assist you," "can I help you on anything else," etc. At the beginning there were negative reactions from some team members, after all it does require a lot of strength to take hits without replying in the same manner. But the team little by little bought the idea and started to seek total satisfaction from our internal customers, many times working until late to address issues of someone in specific, going the extra mile, always with a smile and positive attitude.

The results were not immediate, and many times "negative neighbors" showed up. There were moments when we almost lost our resolve and felt like taking the flowers away from the balcony. But eventually we started getting "thank you" notes, taps on the back, compliments. The arguing started to become less frequent, the lack of respect began to give room to camaraderie and the whole department started to stand out from the crowd. In an internal survey, it was evaluated as excellent and soon some team members received invitations for internal opportunities, including myself. The change in attitude totally paid off and helped our work environment and careers to change substantially.

My perception is that, in our lives, we frequently walk into grey alleys and choose to adapt to it. We get scared of putting our flowers on the balcony, afraid of criticism and simply adopt a defensive attitude. Does it really have to be that way? Can't we just choose to be the agents of change ourselves? Is it absurd to think that we might actually be the ones to give the first step and impact our surroundings with positive energy, bring change and make our balconies flourish? I am positive we are the ones who must take that first step. I am sure that we can make a different choice than accept and adapt to the grey alleys.

I would like to invite you to try this alternative approach to life. Starting today, take with you a contagious smile, a positive attitude, and good vibes. Be a "friend hugger," shake hands with energy, say thank you, treat others with attention and respect, forgive and forget. In summary, put your flowers on the balcony wherever you go. It might take a while, but eventually other balconies will show up. There will be fewer grey alleys and you will have made this world a better and more colorful place.

Parenting In Perspective

"You have to do the best with what God gave you"
Mrs. Gump in the movie "Forrest Gump"

Sometimes, life has to push us out of our center, so we remember what really matters. The example I bring might sound silly, but it did help me put my purpose as a father back in perspective.

Many years ago, my oldest son was in bed with a strong flu that brought in the usual package. Headaches, loss of appetite, some vomiting, and what was most disturbing, a constant high fever that simply would not go away and had him knocked down. We (my wife and I) would medicate him, his temperature would go down a bit, but in a while, it would rise again with full power. The combination of fever with loss of appetite and vomiting got us really worried.

We have been blessed with two very healthy boys, and even when they would catch a cold or flu, they would usually cope well with it, and rarely lost a day in school. So, watching him lying in bed all day, with all that usual energy and vibration transformed into quiet suffering, was a bit of a shock. It changed my mood, my concentration at work wasn't the same, and my patience with day-to-day matters took a vacation.

By now, you must be thinking, "Marcos you overreacted. It was just a strong flu." You might be right, but I believe that a sick son brings back to surface some unresolved issues from my past.

Both our kids were born prematurely, at 31 to 32 weeks of pregnancy. Both spent many days at the intensive care unit. Both times my wife and I went away without taking our babies home, leaving them behind at the hospital so they would receive the needed care and assistance. However, there was an essential difference from one case to the other. The youngest was just taken care of, whereas the oldest was saved. He caught pneumonia right after a very difficult and traumatic delivery, spending his first days fighting for his life. Then, he needed transfusions, took a while to gain weight and just left the hospital after 32 days.

Those 32 days certainly were, and still are, among the most difficult ones in my life. Every night was sleepless, working was inhumanly difficult, music brought no fun, and TV would not distract me.

When he finally went home, one stress went away, but another one began, since I still could not relax. I was bossy over the times for breastfeeding and medicines, I would not allow visitors for a while and when they finally could come, I would make everybody wash their hands with sanitizers before holding him. It took me six months to put me back in balance and be at ease again, assured that our son had come to stay. Before that, we had gone through a year or so trying to get pregnant with no luck.

The bottom line is, I became a father by choice. I really wanted it, but as you might understand by now, it did not come easy. I had to fight for it. And when it finally happened and our baby overcame all hurdles of his difficult start, I made a pact with myself that I would also do everything that depended on me to deserve paternity. At that moment I decided that I was going to be the best father my kids could possibly have and would love them unconditionally. It would not matter if they would be clever or an athlete. What mattered was that they were there, with me, and I would give them all the best a father could give. Leadership, companionship, love. I would be the best example they could have.

As the years pass by, our day-to-day routine takes over, the pressures from our society make their stand, the values start to get all mixed up and we end up losing perspective of what really matters.

In some regretful moment of this story, being among the best in school became more relevant. Being the most important player in the team took priority. Being an example of a kid for the entire world became top of the list. It is impressive how we allow these external pressures to carry us away from our original purposes.

I am very active as a father. I always looked at report cards, went to meetings in school and would not miss a soccer practice. I live the role of a father with great devotion. However, somewhere along the line, my participation no longer became one of mentoring and tutoring. It predominantly became just another point of pressure and criticism.

When we finally got over those days when his health (or the lack of it) got us so worried, I could enjoy once again the pleasant experience of taking him to school and soccer practices. It was an indescribable feeling seeing him back to his day-to-day activities. When I saw him entering the field for another game, the joy was so intense that it literally served me as a slap in the face. And then it hit me. "Yes! That is what really matters. He is with us, and he is healthy. He is here playing, he went to school, he is enjoying his friends. The rest, is just the rest."

Since then, I revised my approach to report cards, soccer games and behaviors that are less than perfect. Instead of being another point of negative pressure, I did my best to be a point of support, guidance, and leadership. I tried to be less critical and more positive in my comments. In summary, I needed to see my treasure at risk, to become once again aware of its real value. I needed that little reminder from life, so I could revive my pact with myself, my original purpose as a father, that had been lost in some bend down the road.

Life has this strange way of communicating with us. Every now and then, it leaves us a note, it hands us a message under the desk, puts a post-it on our computer screen. As a rule, it won't use our common language to express itself. I mean, it is uncommon that someone will tap on your shoulder and say "Dude, you are forgetting this or that. You are not giving the right importance to such and such aspect." Life will talk to us at a different level, using a different protocol. It is our task to read these messages, capture them in the air and make them an opportunity for course corrections, refocus, and go back to our north. Ignoring these messages, these reminders, means we are wasting some golden nuggets. The "divine" (independently of how you understand it) is talking to us and it is our obligation to hear it and translate it, making this divine communication something that helps us steer through the unexpected paths of our lives.

In this results-oriented society, it is so easy to fall for the temptation of dehumanizing our relationships and look at each person that interacts with us through poor and limited lenses. We monetize our employees, we make commerce with our time, we only give attention to those who bring us some benefit, we privilege performance, and forget that we have an essential role as parents, teachers, and leaders, to serve as a lever for the ones we lead (children, students, employees) so they get to the next level.

So, I invite you to think about your relationships and question if you haven't yet fallen for the temptation of making them something poor and dry. If there is something that can be done to improve the way you play your role as parent, teacher, leader, brother, friend.

To close, I recommend you search the internet for some videos of Rick and Dick Hoyt and invest five minutes on this wonderful example of parenting. It is totally worth it.

MAKING THE DIFFERENCE

*"God grant me the serenity to accept the things I
cannot change, the courage to change the things I can,
and the wisdom to know the difference"*

Reinhold Niebuhr

I would like to make use of a story that has circulated on the internet many times, since, given the power of its message, it's always beneficial to revisit. It comes from the book The Star Thrower by Loren Eiseley, and although quite short, it is sure to make us think about the way we interact with the world around us, and with the challenges that life brings to us every now and then. So here goes my free adaptation of it.

Our story is about a writer that used to enjoy early morning walks by the beach, in search of inspiration for his writing.

In a beautiful day, during his walk, he realized the beach was covered by starfish that had been washed upon the shore by a strong tide, and he thought, "the sun is coming up strong; soon they will all dry out and die."

He continued his walk peacefully, until he saw from the distance the figure of a boy that seemed to be quite busy in some sort of difficult task, since he would insist on collecting something from the sand and take whatever it was to the water, time and time again, restlessly.

Curious with such a scene, the writer decided to get closer in order to better understand what was going on. He was quite surprised when he realized that in fact, the boy was throwing starfish by starfish back to the ocean.

With a superior smile on his face, he approached the boy and said:

"Kid, you must have noticed by now that the beach is covered with starfish. Correct?"

The boy, without losing concentration in his task responded briefly.

"Yes!"

The writer kept talking.

"And you must have also noticed that, even if you stay here all day long working as hard as you are, you will not be able to return all starfish that are on the beach, back to the ocean. Right?"

The boy stopped for a moment as if that question had made him think, but he quickly returned to his activity and once again responded.

"Yes!"

Quite surprised by the fact that the boy would not give up on what seemed to be a useless effort, the writer decided to insist on his point, but this time he would be a bit more objective.

"Kid, if you understood that the number of starfish that washed on the beach is almost infinite and that you will not be able to return them all to the ocean, why should you continue? Don't you realize you are not making any difference?"

The boy stopped, looked at the writer, collected another starfish, threw it back to the ocean and said:
"For that one I did."

The boy's answer made him feel a heat wave like those we experience when we do something embarrassing in public. He then remembered his own thought of just a few minutes ago; "soon they will all dry out and die" and reflected on it for a moment. "Where did such indifference come from?"; he asked himself.

Ashamed, he decided to change his own approach to the situation. He reached down to a starfish, threw it back to the ocean and thought, "this one as well, will not die today."

Feeling reenergized by the power of that attitude, he started helping the boy return the starfish to the ocean. That day, writing could wait. A powerful lesson had been learned.

Now, let's stop for a moment and think about this story, since if we analyze it objectively, we will come to the inevitable conclusion that we always make a difference on what surrounds us, one way or another. The question is, what kind of difference do we want to make?

At the beginning, when the writer decided to continue his morning walk, indifferent to the starfish, in his own way he made a difference by not changing anything. Later, when he realized that his perspective was wrong, he made the choice to act and change the fate of, at least, some of the starfish.

When we choose to participate in a donation drive, to support a friend in a difficult moment or a coworker to improve in a new task, on feeding a homeless person in the street, we are making the difference by choosing to make our contribution. When we conveniently think that someone else is already helping or donating, or that the problem is too big and our contribution will be meaningless, we are also making a difference by not changing anything. Being passive is also a choice.

One of the principles of the Theory of Chaos is called the "butterfly effect," which has been subject of films and is abundant in literature. In summary, this principle says that the flapping of the wings of a butterfly, in a chaotic and unpredictable chain of events, may have influence even if very minimum, in the weather or direction of the wind, impacting situations of a much greater scale such as a storm and its effects over a given region.

If we extrapolate this fantastic principle to our lives and our decisions, it might suggest that everything we do (or choose not to do) could have an unimaginable ripple effect in our society and on our planet.

Following this principle, as we encourage a friend or coworker in a new project, he could have a more inspiring day and have an innovative idea that could create new jobs. By helping a person that is going through some difficulties, we could change the direction of this person's life, that could, at that very moment, decide to restart a career, rebuild his life and as a consequence, provide a better life for his kids and grandkids. As we recycle plastic bottles, we could positively impact the environment for centuries.

Quite often in our lives we face problems that, given their magnitude and complexities, make us feel tempted to resign ourselves to the thought that, alone, we won't make much of a difference. Nowadays it is quite common for people to have thoughts such as: "In this place people are so rude, that it's not even worth being courteous." Or "in this Company, everybody is looking out for themselves, so I'm going to protect myself and won't share my knowledge." "The economic problems are so serious that it's not even worth helping the ones in need." As we think this way, we might be wasting great opportunities to create or influence a chain reaction that, on its other end, could be changing a lot of things.

Many people unfortunately believe that changing the world is for dreamers. It's something only to be heard in John Lennon songs (that did change the world, by the way). Well, I have great news for you. You change the world every day, either intentionally or not.

Allow me to introduce a concept in your life. I like to call it "Tangible World." Our tangible world is what surrounds us. Our families, the people we interact with, the company we work for, the community we live in, the schools we go to as students or masters.

It is quite reasonable to think we can't change the whole world, but if we focus in a practical manner on changing our tangible world, we will be changing what is at our reach.

If we dedicate ourselves to our families giving them love, care and guidance, we will be providing a better life for them and the possibilities of a future with expanded horizons. If we make our work environment something more harmonious and positive, if we dedicate ourselves to train and mentor the ones we lead, to have a positive and proactive attitude with our bosses and to be collaborative with our coworkers, we will be making our companies a better workplace. If we share what we have with the less fortunate ones, we will be making their lives a bit better and, in many cases, could actually be saving lives. If we face the fact that, as teachers, we are shaping the future of our students and even of our society, we can make our communities a better one in the decades to come.

It doesn't matter how you look at it, the way we interact with the tangible world is our choice. It is that old, but true saying; you may not be able to control what happens around you, but you most certainly can control how you react to such events.

So, I invite you to reflect on mastering your reactions. You own them. You change the tangible world every moment with them. It is your choice to make the positive difference or not. I invite you to influence, and why not dare to say, to change the tangible world.

You still don't believe you can make a difference? So, let me give you an example based on personal experience.

Not too long ago, I had the pleasure of meeting again a person who had been my intern, many years ago. Together, with the help of other coworkers, we had implemented a set of process metrics and quality reports that were revised on a monthly basis with our customer. I had the opportunity to teach him many things, and since he was a very clever kid, he quickly became very knowledgeable and dominated the subject.

When I asked him what he was doing after all those years, he told me he had become "Master Black Belt" in Quality Management, and that everything had started way back then, with me, in that first professional experience. He then thanked me for the things I taught him and for the good influence I had in his career.

Even today, when I remember that moment, I get emotional.

So, for those who believe that we cannot make a difference, it is my turn to say:

"For this one, I did."

Let's do our part, changing the tangible world for the better, starting today. Leave the rest with the "butterfly effect."

My Musical Rollercoaster

"After silence, that which comes nearest to expressing the inexpressible is music."

Aldous Huxley

People who ride with me in my car constantly ask;, "What is this crazy radio station you are listening to?" To which I jokingly answer: "This is Marcos Rossi FM."
Of course, I'm actually referring to my diverse digital library of songs. Digitalization has changed the musical world. It also changed portability, accessibility, and why not mention, our relationship with our personal music library. Today we can carry in our pockets, wherever we go, the best of our favorite artists. Fantastic!
But the best thing about all this is that this portability has made me more democratic with my own music library. In the old days (I can't help feeling weird about using such words for something that only happened a few years ago), I would carry two or three CDs to the car, which would stay there for several days and, of course, I would give preference to the favorites of the moment. With that,

I would unintentionally leave behind excellent musical material, forgotten on some shelf. They were among the favorites once but would rarely have much playing time again. Today it's all there, in the palm of my hand. All I have to do is press the famous "shuffle" and relax. From that moment on, the device being used is in charge. I let it bring to me, by the rules of chance and the gods of music, whatever it wants, whenever it wants.

Since my music library is quite eclectic in terms of musical genres, time, and place in the world in which the songs were released, by letting the device rule, waiting for the next song becomes a moment of anticipation. You never know what's coming. Like an FM station, except that there are no commercials, and it only plays music that I like. Hence the joke about the Marcos Rossi FM station.

A few years back, I moved far away from my job, and I had a long commute time that I tried to fill out as best I could, sometimes with audiobooks, sometimes with music, or with phone calls to relatives and friends.

During the several minutes that separate origin from destination, when I opt for "my" songs, I enjoy a delightful journey through time and space, with a real roller coaster of rhythms, vibes, and energy. Usually when I arrive, I've listened to more than three languages (I have songs in Portuguese, English, Spanish, Italian, French and some other languages I don't even know what they are); I've traveled back in time several decades (and if I include my classics, we'll have to talk about centuries); I went through various places in the world and transitioned from the agitation of heavy rock, to pop, to dance and romantic, all in a matter of minutes.

So, it is not difficult to understand the restlessness of those who sit with me in the car for some time. It's impossible not to notice that there's something odd about

Flowers on the Balcony

this "radio station." My wife often says she "gets dizzy" with the variations of my songs. And you know what? That's the idea. Listening to music like this makes me have a real mental and emotional gym class. No accommodation or knowing what the next direction is.

I compare that to our lives, since isn't that how things work? If everything we do already had an expected sequence, a repetition of actions and emotions, wouldn't life lose its flavor? Aren't we constantly asked to leave our comfort zone, to seek something new, or to get used to unexpected changes? The truth is that the unexpected always comes, no matter how entrenched we are in our status quo. So, making my musical experience something like a mental and emotional rollercoaster prepares me for these constant changes, which in reality are the only constant in our life.

To better visualize what I mean by this musical roller coaster, imagine a three-dimensional graph. On the horizontal axis is time. When I go from Chuck Berry to Lady Gaga and from Lady Gaga to Led Zeppelin, I travel 70 years forward and then 40 years back. I visualize, and I almost feel like I'm in the fifties, with old cars, typical clothes, and greasy hair. Then I come back to the present and from here I go back to the psychedelic seventies, protesting against some kind of shady power and watching black and white TV, all in less than 10 minutes.

On the vertical axis are the countries of the world. In those forty-five minutes between point A and point B, Eros Ramazzotti takes me to Italy, Al Stewart takes me to Scotland, the Beatles take me to Liverpool, Oasis, to Manchester, Sinatra takes me for a walk in New York; Ivete Sangalo takes me to Bahia, from where Caetano transports me to "Sampa" (São Paulo); Shakira takes me to Colombia, Maná to Mexico; Rush to Canada; Bjork to Iceland; Cranberries to Ireland; Midnight Oil to Australia; Beach

Boys to California; Kitaro to Japan and the Englishman Peter Gabriel, with his fusion of rhythms, takes me to Africa where I meet the Nigerian Sade. All without leaving my car. In the third axis are the most varied rhythms. Chico Buarque brings me samba; Legião Urbana brings me the best that Brazilian rock has ever produced; Renato Teixeira, the best of Brazilian country music; Enya brings me the depth of new age; Narcotango brings me the pop version of tango; Madonna brings me pure pop; Little Richard brings me the old rock and roll; B.B. King brings me the Blues; Spyro Gyra brings me modern jazz while Traditional Jazz Band takes me back to the roots of that same rhythm; Mozart brings me the classical; Shania Twain, the country and Dave Matthews Band, the fusion of almost all the above.

If you could imagine this three-dimensional chart, imagine what it is like to transition in a matter of seconds, from England of the 1960s to Brazil of the 1990s, transported by the rock of the Rolling Stones and the MPB of Marisa Monte, and from there we jump into an abrupt turn to the 1970s in Australia with the romanticism of the Bee Gees, and from there to the United States of the last decades, with the rock fusion of Linkin Park. Can you understand the roller coaster?

If we add to all this, the most varied emotions and messages brought by each of these three-dimensional turns, the feeling can be none other than that of a roller coaster worthy of a Disney Park. Some examples: Joe Satriani makes me feel like I'm flying (and I'm in the car at 90 miles per hour, so, imagine the danger), Alanis Morrissette's dualities make me think about my own; The Allman Brothers make me play imaginary guitar (yes, I know, I'm driving); Andrea Bocelli makes me believe that I can sing opera (of course, in Italian); Barry Manilow reminds me that I'm always ready to try again (Ready to Take a Chance

Again); Boston tells me not to look back, that a new day is breaking (Don't Look Back); while Beto Guedes reminds me that all love is sacred, and Seal reinforces it soon after, saying that love is divine. Black Eyed Peas makes me believe that the night is going to be good; Gonzaguinha screams at me saying that life is beautiful, and soon after comes Louis Armstrong telling me that this is a wonderful world. Then Bruce convinces me that everyone has a hungry heart and Charlotte Church makes me pray with Pie Jesu. Next comes 14 Bis and reminds me that I am a hunter of myself; U2 makes me scream that it's a beautiful day (even if it's raining) and, along with The Corrs, make me want to be Irish at least for a day. Tina Turner convinces me that I'm simply the best and Pink Floyd's guitar makes me believe I've entered another dimension. Skank reminds me how beautiful a football match is; and Queen reminds me that we are the champions, even if you are a Dolphins fan. But not everything is joy, since The Police reminds me that I'm the King of Pain; the Smiths make me feel melancholic (in the rain on a Manchester corner) and Joy Division takes me to rock bottom. But soon comes Pet Shop Boys and New Order rescuing me and making me want to dance in the middle of the Turnpike, followed by Jota Quest with an easy song to sing along. And then, here comes John Lennon making a dreamer of me; Gianluca Grignani reminds me of my son; David Bowie makes me play drums on the car wheel with Modern Love; but soon comes Loreena Mckennitt and takes me into the Celtic world and relaxes me.

Well, I could stay on this three-dimensional trip of different emotions and vibes for hours (and sometimes I do), but I think you got the idea.

To give a colorful end to this musical journey, I recommend that you search the Internet for the music video "Stand by Me" of the Playing for Change movement, which shows the universality of music, and that you do not have to be a Broadway star to put up a show.

When life changes rhythm from one moment to the next without warning you, sing and dance to the new song. It will soon be followed by another, and then another and another, and it is not for us to know what rhythm they will bring us.

Keep singing and dancing. The unexpected always comes!

The Love Proposition

*"Spread love everywhere you go.
Let no one ever come to you without leaving
happier than they were before."*
Madre Tereza of Calcutta

Some time ago, I made an analogy between a management concept and our daily lives, which led me to see the way I interact with people around me from a somewhat different perspective. Please allow me to share this concept with you.

In the Corporate world, especially in companies that are essentially service providers, there is a very powerful concept that helps them focusing on their relationships with their current customers and also to make more compelling service offerings to potential new ones. This concept is called the Value Proposition.

Over a very detailed analysis of the value a given service company is willing to create to its customers, sometimes even measured in financial terms, it becomes much easier and more objective to demonstrate that a given relationship is worth having and is actually beneficial to both.

Many times, during their lives, organizations question their relationships and the benefit of keeping them, finishing them, or even enhancing them. Customers in general question if the money invested in the services being rendered to them is something that is still bringing the expected benefits. If the service provider is not bringing to the table something relevant and is unable to show, in a very practical and objective way, what is the value being added, many times these relationships come to an end. For that reason, a service provider must be constantly reviewing and questioning its value proposition to each of its customers, so it may periodically recreate and renovate this proposal and continue to bring something new to these relationships, making their customers continuously interested in keeping them.

Over time, companies change. By internal and external pressures their priorities are revised, their target customers change, their strategies and tactical efforts are redirected. Often, they also change their products and, consequently, their needs as customers towards their own suppliers are also reviewed. For these reasons, during the relationship between two companies, the value proposition must be constantly revisited. Commonly, a mature organization will have different expectations from its suppliers than a young one would. An organization that is going through some financial difficulties could even have other necessities that could be more related to their survival. Therefore, another thing to be taken into consideration is the maturity level of the customer, its moment in terms of success or failure and obviously, the maturity of the relationship between the companies involved.

Finally, analyzing the value proposition from a potential supplier, helps companies select service providers in a way that enables them to bring to their business what is more beneficial for their growth, or for them to stabilize and keep themselves alive in the market in a competitive manner.

By now, after reading these half a dozen paragraphs, you must be thinking: Ok Marcos, this is all really interesting, but what does any of that have to do with me?

Well, one of these days I was questioning myself about what drives us, sometimes on a very intuitive level, to the conclusion that this or that person is good or interesting for us to get closer to? Why, so many times, do we decide to keep a reasonable distance from this or that person? Why would it be, that there are people that are practically "irresistible." They attract us and make us get closer and closer, until we realize we have opened our doors to such person in a way that they become an important part of our lives, with a free pass to provide opinions, suggestions, advice and to share our moments of joy and pain. They are always there in a positive way, helping us grow, elevating us, making us feel better than we were before their appearance. Everybody knows someone like that.

Now think about these people, about their actions, gestures, their attitude to life, their honest interest in knowing how you feel, but think mostly about the way they look at you. As the saying goes, the eyes are the mirror of the soul. Those who look you in the eye, fear not to show what they bring inside.

In general, these people have something different that makes us feel good in their presence. These people bring with them, although not materialized in a piece of paper or in numbers, a compelling proposition; a compelling, although implicit, love proposition.

When I had this thought a few days ago, it was like having a revelation. Either if it is something explicit, something that we can feel in the air, or even in the energy of each person, every one of us bring along a love proposition to the people around us, such as our spouses, our kids, our parents, relatives, friends, neighbors, pets, people that cross our ways in the streets and even to our planet. And you know what? We bring a love proposition even to our rivals and enemies. We bring in our hearts a love proposition to the whole world around us.

Bible experts say that many original messages from Jesus ended up having a different meaning, given some inaccurate translations attributed to what he preached. One of these transformations happened to the concept of loving everyone, even your enemies. Nowadays we have in the word love essentially an emotional meaning that makes it something you feel, not something you practice. That being said, feeling love for someone I don't know or for somebody that is my enemy is something simply not viable. How could any individual possibly nurture such noble feelings for someone they already feel resentment or even in many cases, hate?

In Jesus times, it was quite common for people to write in Greek, considered the most erudite of the languages and therefore, almost of mandatory knowledge for those few who knew how to write or read. In Greek, there are three different words for what we conventionally call love these days. There is the word "Eros" that has a more erotic and sexual orientation. There is the word "Storge" with a meaning connected to the affection we have for people that are dear to us, and finally there is the word "Agape."

The verb "Agape" talks about what we unconditionally practice in terms of doing good things to others, independently of their culture, race, religion and also independently of what they represent to us emotionally speaking. According to these Bible experts, every time the gospels describe the situations when Jesus spoke about loving your dear ones, your neighbors or even your enemies, the word originally used was "Agape," what suggests we should rethink these teachings. In other words, it suggests that Jesus did not expect us to feel love for people we don't know or for someone that was not dear to us. Jesus meant that we shall practice love towards everyone and everything. With this new meaning in mind, love is not what one feels. Love is what one does. What we do to others is what really matters.

Following this line of thought, it becomes possible to love anybody. We may love the people that we actually feel love for, and we can love the people that we should practice love to. And that brings us back to the proposition talk.

What kind of love proposition do we bring to our life partners? How do we exercise love with them day to day? What do we bring to the table in this relationship? Do we keep in perspective the needs of the person involved? Do we try to keep them not only satisfied but happy by having our presence around? Do we work to make the relationship something worth having every moment? Do we try to periodically evaluate their life moments, their ages, their pressures, anxieties, pain points and values? Do we try to make these people feel loved in such a way that it becomes unnecessary for them to search for other relationships that may bring a more interesting love proposition for their specific life stages and needs?

How is our love proposition to our kids doing? Are we providing them with what they need as human beings, as people that need our care and attention, as well as our leadership as parents? Could it be that our love proposition is just focusing on school grades and what they will be when they grow up? What have we done in order to make our love proposition to be enough, so these very special people don't feel lonely, misunderstood, isolated, and don't feel like going out there searching for adventure in the world of addictions? Is our love proposition helping them grow in a balanced manner? Is it teaching them to nurture love and take positive energy and vibes to the world out there?

What do we say about our love proposition to the people we work with? Could it be that we are bringing to the table just a pragmatic proposal of a poor and dry "give and take" that transforms these relationships into something easy to replace? What are we adding to the ones we lead? What have we done to make them grow and be something better than they were when we first met them?

And what about our parents, relatives, neighbors, and people that we meet on the streets? If love is what one does, we can love each and every one of these individuals and bring something good to them. And how is our love proposition to people we don't even know? And what to say about our rivals, don't they deserve at least humane and respectful treatment? What about the animals and nature? What about our planet? What is our love proposition to everything that is given to us by our divine Father?

Bottom line my friends, our love proposition is already there rather we know it objectively or not. As we come to be aware of its existence, it becomes our prerogative to revise it, refine it, improve it, and align it to the needs of each person involved in our relationships, so they can actually feel loved. It can also be taught as a concept to our kids at a young age, so it may help them frame it, manage it and later in their lives, learn to recognize it in the eyes of other people. We may also use this concept to identify the people who bring in their eyes selfish and stingy love propositions, so these people may be carefully avoided and placed in a secondary relevance in our lives, preventing us from having many disappointments. Last, but not least, we should be constantly revising the love propositions that the people around us are offering to us. Are the love propositions being offered by our spouses really what we need, deserve, and expect from them? If not, we can use this concept to realign and improve our relationships. What about our friends, relatives, coworkers, neighbors? We can use this to objectively improve all of our relationships, or if the case, as a matter of last resource, replace some of them. There are many interesting love propositions out there.

So, let's keep in mind that love is what one does and let's practice it more often, exercising it in every situation of our lives.

Waking up this morning at 5 AM to share these thoughts with you is my "Agape" gesture of the day.

THE "LUCCA-PETO" BALANCE

"If you tighten the strings too much, they will snap, and if you leave them too loose, they won't play—The path to enlightenment is in the middle way."

Siddhartha in the movie *"Little Buddha"*

I have two sons named Gianlucca and Gianpietro (who I affectionately call "Peto"). Although they look very much alike physically, they are very different in their personalities and in their approach to life and day-to-day situations.

While Gianlucca, the oldest, was more restrained in his dealings with strangers, Gianpietro, the youngest, was more extroverted and made new friends quickly. While Gianlucca was always trying to stand out by his athletic and academic abilities, Gianpietro was seeking notoriety by his constant sense of humor, spreading a good vibe with his jokes and funny moves. In the end, both achieved academic and sportive success, as well as popularity, but with quite different approaches.

But what always struck me most about their differences was that one was more competitive and the other just wanted to have a good time. While the first wanted to be among the best of his classroom and be the captain of the team, the other wanted more to entertain himself, have a good laugh, and as long as he achieved a positive participation with good grades and well-played games, he would happily move on with his life.

It was quite amusing to watch them play video games. They would usually start quite well, but soon this initial harmony would come to an end, since while Gianlucca was playing to win, overcome obstacles and pass to the next level, Gianpietro was just having fun and would start with his jokes and pranks. When crisis was about to set in and they were about to jump on each other, I would intervene to restore peace.

Often times, I advised them to review these behaviors and start seeking a balance where Gianlucca could be less rigid and competitive and Gianpietro could be more serious and learn that when we are doing something as a team, success depends on a good participation of each of the members, doing what they have to do. One should seek success, but having fun along the way, while the other should have fun, seeking success along the way. If each of them could move a little bit in the direction of the other, video games would surely be much more peaceful and fun for both.

And come to think of it, I believe that those conversations were good for their development, as they both grew up to become more balanced as adults.

Reflecting on this, I began to extrapolate this antagonism to our day-to-day life, since we are often required to act with extreme seriousness and competitiveness, leaving little time to laugh, have fun, relax, and enjoy the moment. When we have some play time and do not need to be efficient, we often navigate to the other extreme, sometimes seeking relief on the consumption of alcohol (or worse), shutting down the engines entirely, not producing anything creative and allowing laziness to take over. Or we even take the competitive edge to the extreme on activities that should be relaxing, like that after-work soccer match among friends, where suddenly winning is all that matters, and friendship is placed in the back seat. On the other hand, some individuals are just overly relaxed, and take nothing seriously, many times compromising important team efforts, allowing great life changing opportunities to slip away, simply because they are on a constant "don't worry be happy" state of mind.

For these and many other reasons, I believe it is important to seek balance, being serious when we are supposed to be, but not forgetting to smile and have fun with teammates, looking at our failures as a learning process of life, something temporary to be overcome in the next attempt or new project. And when we have an opportunity to have fun, we should enjoy the moment without the need of anesthetics of any kind, always seeking a positive participation, contributing to the wellbeing of all in a healthy moment of pleasure.

Since I had such reflections, I started calling this balance I seek, the "Lucca-Peto" balance, as a tribute to my beloved sons. Now, every time I see myself taking things a bit too seriously, I think of my Gianpietro with his loud and uncontained laughing and the adorable gift of smiling back to life, recovering in a quite light and unattached manner when things don't go his way. And when I notice myself more relaxed than I should be, I remember my Gianlucca and his passionate way of giving his best in his soccer games, even when the match is already lost, and his constant search for excellence in his school grades.

As a matter of fact, seeking balance and avoiding the extremes is not a new concept in my life. This is an old Buddhist concept that I carry along since my early twenties.

"Seek the middle way." I always try to balance the time dedicated to work with the time dedicated to taking good care of the mind, body, and soul. I try to find time to be with family and friends, but I also seek time to be with myself. Although I cannot help feeling like I'm running around trying to balance many spinning plates, I believe I haven't dropped anyone so far. Sometimes one of them will shake and dance like it is about to fall, but the side effects of me neglecting that falling plate will soon be felt and I run to swirl it around until it is rotating again.

If I read little, my mind gets rusty. If I don't exercise my body aches and complains. If I am far from God, my soul hardens. If I work little, tasks will pile up. On the other hand, if I read too much, I don't find time to exercise. If I exercise too much, I don't pray enough. If I just mind the spirit, I don't read. And if I work too much, I don't find time to do all these other things.

If I seek too much privacy, I isolate myself from family and friends. If I stay only with my family, I don't see my friends and if I stay only with my friends, I don't have time to enjoy my family. And if I only dedicate time to friends and family, I don't find time for my meditation moments and consequently I will find no inspiration to write.

Once I heard from a consultant that balance is an overrated concept, since people that reach greatness do not prioritize living a balanced life. Following that line of thought, if you want to be a great musician, you must dedicate yourself to music all the time. If you want to be a great athlete, you must leave and breathe the physical activity of your choice. If you want to be a great entrepreneur, you must dedicate yourself to your business 24 hours a day, 7 days a week.

You know what? The consultant is absolutely right. He only forgot to mention that in many of those success cases, these high-performance achievers live unhappy lives on their way to glory. It wouldn't come as a surprise if that athlete raising the trophy had limited time with his/her children, did not know much of the world and lives a nomad life that does not allow him/her to cultivate family and deepen friendships. The same thing applies to famous musicians, since it is quite common for these examples of success to have a history of drug abuse, doping and other additives. Some successful executives or entrepreneurs might as well look at their great bank account and say, I won. But then I ask, after how many divorces? In these cases of extreme dedication to a cause or career I frequently ask myself if they would remember their children's kindergarten graduations. And what's worse; would their children remember their busy parents having consistent positive participation in their important moments? We quite commonly hear stories of great athletes being involved in doping scandals, famous musicians becoming drug addicts, and high executives or entrepreneurs living lonely lives.

Of course, there are many cases of successful people that were able to manage staying away from drugs, alcohol, and at the same time, were also successful on building fortune and solid, stable families. To them I surely take my hat off. But for me, the risks involved are not worth it. I refuse to prioritize public success, notoriety, or financial fortune since for me they are nothing but dangerous illusions.

So, for these and other reasons, I prefer to follow my philosophy of the "Lucca-Peto Balance," seeking the middle way. Not so serious, but not so relaxed. Not overly competitive, but not indifferent as well. Not prioritizing fortune but neither trying to become a monk. Always reading, but also taking care of my physical and mental health.

I will keep turning and balancing my plates. There must be time for everything in life; even time to share these thoughts with you.

DOING GOOD DEEDS BECAUSE WE MUST

"Kindness, selflessness and generosity are not the exclusive property of any race or religion."
Gandhi

A few years ago, a good friend of mine shared with me some thoughts questioning the habit of doing good deeds to others, which ended up triggering an interesting exchange of emails between us.

She questioned the fact that, in some situations of our lives, we do something good for others just because we believe it is the right thing to do, but sometimes we are not emotionally aligned with such gestures. As an example, she mentioned giving food to a homeless person while wishing he would be gone, away from her doorway, since his presence made her uncomfortable. She asked me if that thought alone wasn't already a sin. With her permission I will share part of this conversation and will elaborate a bit more on the subject.

The first suggestion I made was for her to leave aside the whole thing about being a sinner in these cases, since if we take this concept of sinning by our thoughts too seriously, we will all be damned to eternal fire. There would be no salvation. The human being is so full of dualities and defenses, that thoughts which could be considered not so elevated, populate our minds with greater frequency than we would like to admit. I believe that it is part of human nature to look over each situation from many different angles. We are contradictory by nature and still bring inside of us the genetic heritage of a primitive beast that articulates defensive thoughts in order to feel protected from external threats. And what we might consider a potential threat could be so many things.

When we are little, we are "programed" by the world around us to like or dislike things, people, situations, and behaviors. We take that "program" along for years and years until one day, as adults, we become mature enough to rationalize and revise them, since they might be no longer the most adequate ones.

Let's stop for a moment and think about this genetic aspect that I just mentioned. Inside our evolutionary heritage we bring along everything we once were. When I was a teenager, I read the book Cosmos by Carl Sagan. At some point, he mentions that our brains carry different evolutionary layers, being the most primitive very similar to the brain of a reptile, making us very territorial, protecting our space and keeping an innate aggressiveness against everything that threatens us. Over this "alligator brain" we have something similar to a mammal brain. It makes us caretakers of our offspring, as a lioness takes care of her cubs. At last, we have the cortex, the most evolved and rational part of our brains. And what is most interesting about all this is that these three layers that work in very different ways, are still functioning, and every now and then, get in conflict with each other. Have you ever noticed that when you are all alone in an elevator and somebody comes in, we tend to split the available space in half? And if there are four people, we position ourselves one in each corner? And if someone we don't know gets too close, we back up a bit? And we do all that without rationalizing it. This is all part of our primitive defense mechanisms. These same primitive instincts impel us to procreation in order to perpetuate our species, and also make us look at people of the opposite sex as they pass, with an interest that is not always the most adequate to modern day standards. Evidently this impulse is not very successful with the most jealous partners. But the fact is that all these things operate at irrational levels that we do not fully control, and willing to eliminate them from our behaviors would be a noble, but very unrealistic intention. That all being said, I suggest we put aside this matter of judging ourselves for our thoughts and instinctive reactions, since it is not at this level that most of our decisions are made. For that we have the cortex, privilege of the human species, which serves well for the rationalization and control of all these processes I just mentioned.

Now let's think a bit about our educational and cultural heritages. When we are little, we are taught different types of values and behaviors that will influence us for years and years. Our parents, teachers, relatives, older friends, mass communication vehicles, they all provide us with the most diverse points of reference, which many times we adopt for the rest of our lives. We end up creating frames of references to fit people from other cultures, religions, races, sexual orientation, and social levels.

When I was a child, I grew up in small countryside towns that were part of a Brazilian society where African descendants were very few and most commonly very poor and less educated; people with leftist points of view were persecuted; homosexuals were mistreated and segregated; and the only religious option around was Catholicism. I carried those points of reference for years, until I questioned and revised them. Depending on what was taught by all the agents described above to this friend of mine when she was little, it is more than natural that she would still have on her mind some defense mechanisms with the homeless person, maybe by judging him less clean, possibly carrying some contagious disease, or even as a threat to her physical integrity.

In summary, for us to better understand these dualities, it is necessary to put in perspective our instinctive filters and cultural heritages. Judging ourselves as sinners by one thought or another, which has roots in the depths of our psyche, is unfair to say the least. This is all part of being humans, thinking animals living in a society in constant mutation, that revises its own values with the passing of time. The question at hand goes far beyond religious aspects.

For centuries, the matter of loving your neighbor and doing good deeds for others has been a privilege of religious discussions, when in fact in my opinion, it should not be that way. Unfortunately, our schools do not teach us how to handle our relationships in a harmonic way and, even less so, in a loving way. Many times, even at home in our family lives, such things are not taught. These subjects end up being discussed only at the churches and temples, and that is such a shame. I have been reviewing that myself for quite some time now, and today my understanding is that doing good deeds and helping other people is much more an ethical matter, as it is also a matter of survival for the human species, than a religious discussion. We shouldn't need to believe in this or that religion in order to wish well and do good deeds for other human beings, help one another and, why not, to love one another. This approach, that should be part of our family and formal educations, unfortunately is so rare among us, that when someone openly preaches about it in a consistent and vehement way, thy person ends up becoming a priest, a nun or even candidate for canonization.

I believe that doing good deeds and helping other people should be a matter of a rational choice. Think about it. What are the alternatives? Turn our backs to people in need (like the homeless person)? Segregation of all kinds and sorts because of race, color of the skin, different religion, foreign culture, and other sexual orientation? Selfishness, thinking only about ourselves and not sharing what we have with less fortunate ones? Being limited to a territorial and competitive being as our primitive ancestors once were? Being sexually instinctive, offending and even violating the moral and physiological integrity of a woman or a child? Seek domination over a different geographical area, subjugating other peoples and cultures (also known as war)? If we stop to think of where these roads will lead us, we will only reach one destination: evil, violence and self-destruction. Do we really need to get into religious discussions to realize something so obvious?

Please, do not get me wrong. I am not defending a "no religion" approach to life. That is not the point. I know from experience that in general, a religion is a good thing for people, and commonly ends up playing the role of a catalyst for this aspiration of doing good deeds to others, and sharing what we have with the less fortunate ones. I just think that religions could give a little more emphasis to spiritual elevation, helping us not becoming so materialists, less attached to possessions and lead us closer to a divine experience, aspects many times relegated to a secondary role during rites and cults. My point is, independently of the religious aspects of the matter, we should do good deeds to others simply because the alternatives are a disaster.

At the end of the dialogue with my friend, I suggested she should release herself from the weight and the need to like the homeless person. Just reinforcing what I've already said in the essay The Love Proposition, love is what one does not what one feels. I finished by saying that if she could at least feel compassion for him, she would have evolved quite a bit as a human being. For that to be possible, we need to develop something called empathy. We need to put ourselves in the place of others and try to feel what they feel, think with their heads; understand their educational and cultural heritages, and even their spiritual legacies. That homeless person could have quite a story to tell.

When younger, I did some voluntary work at a shelter for elderly people in Campinas, Brazil. Old men and women, many times abandoned by their families and by life itself, shared a little of their life experiences with me and that was a unique experience in my life. Many had been artists, worked in companies, and once had lives like yours or mine. But things changed and there they were, without anybody else but their own selves, helping one another in the last years of their lives. The homeless person could very well have a similar story. You can be sure that, in most cases, being a homeless person was more of a consequence, not a choice.

Helping others just for the sake of having a lighter conscience obviously is not the best of options available, but it's better than doing nothing at all. It is also important to give or help someone without fostering superiority. We should not position ourselves as superiors. In each of the extremities between a helper and someone being helped, there could be just a matter of luck, time, and spiritual legacy, which orchestrates things in levels that are yet beyond our understanding. We shall look at the helped one at the same level and with compassion for the unfortunate moment such a person is going through. Come tomorrow and this could all be different, and we could be in the opposite extremes.

As a reflection about all this, I suggest we should not be as harsh on ourselves when it comes down to our thoughts, which many times have their genesis on mental and psychological levels that we do not fully control. We shall understand ourselves less as sinners but more as human beings, incomplete and full of flaws, but eternally in evolution. What matters is that we must rationalize such not so noble thoughts and decide in a confident and conscious way to help and do good deeds to others, simply because it's worth it. And we shall not do it in order to earn points in heaven, so we come to deserve a far distant idealized post-mortem paradise, but to create a better world now. The alternative to such an approach just pushes us apart from each other and leads us towards selfishness, isolation, solitude and, in extremes, to violence, war, and self-extermination.

Let's do good deeds to others simply because we must and that's it. The rest is philosophical discussion. And by the way, have you done something good to others today? What are you waiting for?

Cultivating The Garden of The Mind

"A man is but the product of his thoughts. What he thinks, he becomes."
Gandhi

Many years ago, my oldest son asked me if we could have a little talk. He came to me with his best 11-year-old "young adult" look in his eyes and said, "Dad, can we talk just the two of us for a moment?"

I promptly attended to his request but got kind of worried when we pulled me to the office and closed the door behind us. I thought to myself; "Oh my! What could be going on here?"

Then he began to articulate his best arguments and justifications to try to convince me that he was already old enough to have this video game where you carry a gun to kill zombies, and since he was the only one among his friends who did not have it, he was feeling somewhat behind and inferior.

With a deep breath of relief, since I thought this could be something much more serious, I treated the subject calmly, with the necessary care and attention.

The issue is that my wife and I have always carried a pacifist philosophy. We are antiviolence in general and contrary to the use of fire weapons. We do not have them at home or in the car and we try to prevent our kids from having access to toys that suggest violence. On their birthdays we always requested our guests to avoid giving them toy guns or war like games or figures, soldier forts or things of the like. As they grew up, we have applied the same orientation to video games. We do not allow war or fighting games that replicate violence. Therefore, for obvious reasons, a game where you carry a gun to kill zombies is kind of out of the question.

It's not that we are trying to raise our kids in a bubble, away from the realities we have out there. We know it will be unavoidable that they play soldier or cop and robber with their friends, and even that they play these video games when visiting one of them. We just want to send the message that, in our values scale, these attitudes and role plays are not the best influence, and that we shall always be in search of a more peaceful and healthier world, nurturing on them a reflection about these matters since they are little.

That day, in my conversation with my oldest, I told him I understood quite well his discomfort about feeling behind, but that this was a problem he would have to learn to deal with, since other differences would eventually appear as time would go by, which not always we would be able to level up. As a matter of fact, some of these differences were actually good to experience. They were even necessary. I also told him that I would rather see him facing this type of difficulty, than to have his mind poisoned by these violent images, killing monsters for hours on end. It was then that I introduced to him the metaphor in which our minds are like gardens, with very fertile soil and whatever we plant and nurture there will grow, a metaphor that I would like to explore a little more with you.

This metaphor is not new or original. It's been around for thousands of years and finds its roots in the Far East cultures. It was recently explored in the book The Monk Who Sold His Ferrari by Robin Sharma, where the author makes use of a number of metaphors to suggest some practices and attitudes that may contribute to make our lives healthier and more balanced.

In the book, Robin uses one of his characters to explore the concept that our minds are like gardens that must be cultivated every day and every moment. If we do not take good care of our garden and allow anything to be planted and cultivated, or trash to be thrown at it, soon it will be full of weeds, bugs, and dirt, which will little by little suffocate and kill all beautiful plants and flowers. Our garden will soon have nothing to show of beauty and will become just a pile of trash and weeds.

On the other hand, if we take good care of our garden daily, cleaning it, cultivating the flowers, pulling out the weeds, killing the intruding bugs and plagues, it will quickly flourish and stand out as a pleasant spectacle of colors and aromas to our senses and spirit.

Our minds are just like that. We shall consistently watch our thoughts cultivating what is good and positive, while we extract what is destructive and negative. The constant exercise of positive thinking and good attitudes contribute to a much healthier mind and consequently, better lives. There is abundant literature about the influence that positive thinking and attitude can have in our lives.

However, I would like to approach this subject from a different angle. We shall also impose constant surveillance of what we grant permission to enter into our minds. If we do not police our constant exposure to images, sounds and literature filled with bad energy, which unfortunately also exists in abundance around us, these bad vibes will begin to grow roots and influence our thoughts. In the long run they could also start to shape our behaviors, our character and finally, our destiny.

We are bombarded daily by television with journalistic images which are trying to make a sensation out of everything that is bad in our society. Unfortunately, good examples and behaviors become news less often than they should. As a consequence, we end up watching for hours and hours a parade of bad examples of all sorts, occupying the noble hours of our time and attention. We can see the same patterns of behavior when, only by the end of a film or show, the villain gets caught or killed. But not before they spent hours (or even months, if it's a series) sending all sorts of wrong messages about how to make a living, on how to get the attention of the prettiest girls or handsome guys, driving around in a fashionable sports car.

In the media in general, what we see, time and time again, is the success of musical groups or singers that have very little of substance to say and, in many circumstances, know absolutely nothing about music, but have videos and choreographies full of sensual content that show the supposed "artists" driving the best cars, and going out with the prettiest ladies that shake their behinds in front of the cameras the whole time.

Horror or action movies are typically full of unnecessary violence, that suggest revenge and justice made with own hands, full of weapons of the latest technology. They all end up promoting that same behavior, which may as well be repeated in the streets and homes of a lot of people.

And evidently, we shall not forget to mention some video games that tend to transform the players in addicts, spending hours and hours repeating the same patterns of behavior, killing, committing acts of violence, destroying things, running away from the police, or even annihilating it in a brutal fashion.

If we allow our minds to be invaded by all these types of images, reading material and sounds that I just mentioned, the results will most likely not be positive. The effects of this visual and audio poisoning in our brains in the long run are hard to dimension, but they certainly influence our thoughts, and our thoughts end up influencing our lives.

What I suggest as an alternative for this defenseless constant exposure to these images, literature and sounds which end up contaminating our mental gardens is nothing radical like living in a bubble, turning off our televisions and computers. It is a very simple but powerful concept that can make a substantial difference in our lives and is based on an analogy of a common day-to-day practice. It is the concept of the door viewer. Those small little holes we have in our doors with amplifying lenses which allow us to see who is outside of our doorways.

When somebody rings the bell of your home, do you simply come and open the door allowing whoever is out there to come in and then you ask what the person wants? Of course, you don't. First you look through the door viewer, trying to identify the person. And if you do not know him/her, you try to find out who the person is and what are his/her intentions, so you may be in position to make a better judgment if you should open the door or not. Once you open the door, other questions will come until you feel comfortable about letting the person in. When that stranger is finally in, he/she will still be observed closely for a while until you relax and feel secure that there are no risks or bad intentions, and you can finally make the person feel welcome and at home.

Have you noticed that this act of safety we apply almost mechanically and intuitively is not similarly applied with what comes in through the doors of our televisions, cell phones and computers? These electronic doors are almost invariably open, and we end up accepting any intruders, not questioning why they came, what is their purpose and if they will bring good or bad things to us.

What if you apply the door viewer concept and search for information on what are the purposes of the "intruders," questioning what their intentions and objectives are before you invite them into your home? If the "intruders" convince you that they should be invited in, don't bring your defenses down just yet. Put them to test and check if what is brought to you is made of good or bad vibes and messages, if it stimulates good thoughts and examples. Only if the "intruders" pass all these tests, they should receive your welcome and be allowed to be part of your life.

As I closed my conversation with my son that day, making use of this metaphor, he understood my position and, although not too happy with the outcome, gave me a hug and thanked me for my care and attention.

Later that night at church, he had his communion for the first time by my side and knelt down for his prayers. I could not hold the tears which came from the emotion of seeing him growing and completing one more stage of his evolution as a person. In that moment I felt assured I had fulfilled my role as a father, scoring one more point towards making both my sons two healthy human beings, with a positive attitude towards life.

To close our subject, I suggest we start using door viewers over what influences our thoughts and the thoughts of the ones we love. Let's cultivate the gardens of our minds. Let's cultivate more flowers in it. The world out there is in desperate need of beautiful balconies.

OUR DAILY AGNUS DEI

"All major religious traditions carry basically the same message; that is love, compassion, and forgiveness. The important thing is that they should be part of our daily lives."
Dalai Lama

As we go through our busy and stressful schedules of our day-to-day, we are sometimes blessed with soothing and relaxing moments, which carry the gift of opening a straight connection with what is divine, with what comes from the powers of creation, with what is from above (doesn't matter how you understand it). Since we are constantly running and our minds are always busy with concerns of all kinds, we end up shifting our attentions away from these spiritual portals that open right in front of us. We make the mistake of restricting ourselves by only opening this connection with what is divine when we are in some sort of cult, mass or when we are praying, therefore losing great opportunities to keep it open more frequently.

These moments usually manifest themselves in the simplest things, such as when we are watching the sunrise or sunset, when we observe the full moon shining over a lake, when we see a white heron gracefully spread the wings and fly, as we witness somebody doing a nice gesture, when we receive some sort of grace, when we meet someone special for us or even when we experience a moment of affection from someone we love. All these situations are opportunities to exercise this connection with the divine and live in constant communion with what is beyond our humble comprehension. In fact, in moments like these, the understanding of this energy is something irrelevant. What really matters when such a connection is established, is to open this channel of communication with our creator and feel this beautiful moment, make it strong, be thankful and elevate our spirits.

What also has the power of opening these magical portals with divine energy is music. The "Ave Maria" of Gounod or Schubert are great examples. All you have to do is close your eyes and feel the vibes in order to get yourself spiritually elevated.

However, the song that easily elevates me spiritually and quickly connects me with divine vibes is Pie Jesu. It doesn't matter if it is being interpreted by Charlotte Church or Sarah Brightman. Whenever I listen to it, I really let it in, I feel each vibe, every voice intonation, every musical note, and I immediately connect with what is most divine. I feel very close to the powers of creation. It is like this power and I are one, even if for a brief moment.

The words of the song say:

"Pie Jesu, Qui tollis peccata mundi; Dona eis réquiem, Agnus Dei, Qui tollis peccata mundi; Dona eis réquiem"

At the mass, these verses are recited or sang every Sunday, as we ask to the "Lamb of God (Agnus Dei), who takes away the sins of the world, to grant us peace and rest."

The idea of having an omnipotent source of love and

energy that takes away what is evil in us, that forgives our imperfections and grants us peace, is quite comforting. These verses are usually sung in beautiful melodies, that touch me deeply, taking me and this divine energy to a deep communion.

It doesn't really matter who sings it. What is really strong about these centuries old verses is the concept that there is always the possibility of getting spiritually purified, of making a total cleaning of our souls, since there is an "Agnus Dei" that takes from us what is bad, that gives us peace, but most importantly, that forgives our imperfections.

I think we actually fail to realize how strong this concept is. Do we ever stop to consider the possibility that we might have the power and plenty of opportunities to incorporate this in our lives? That we may as well become a source of redemption and spiritual elevation for the ones around us?

I believe we all carry the gift of potentially being the "Agnus Dei" of someone, even if for a brief moment, taking away what is negative in a relationship, forgiving imperfections, granting peace.

The power of forgiveness, the honest pardoning that comes from the heart, is possibly the supreme source of redemption for our relationships with the ones we deeply care about. It's what strengthens the connections, is what allows us to move ahead, what brings peace among people.

Let's stop for a moment and think about how we complicate our relationships given the incredible difficulty we usually have in forgiving the imperfections of others.

In the relationship of a couple, acceptance of one another's imperfections is a common struggle. It is difficult to manage the differences and understand the other as an incomplete, work-in-process human being, who will certainly make mistakes, but also deserves our compassion and our forgiveness for such imperfections. The values of modern society impel us to be more and more strict and inflexible with others, leading us to focus on other people's mistakes, demanding apologies, and corrective actions, creating more and more disagreements and arguments. If by the end of these arguments the couple does not exercise the "Agnus Dei," forgiving one another, redeeming the relationship, and taking away what is hurting, bringing peace to one another, the arguing will be of no benefit and the macules will remain there, waiting for the next chance to strike back and resuscitate painful discussions, bringing more disagreements and little by little weakening the bonds of the relationship.

Among parents and their kids, the conflicts of generations usually steal the best years of these relationships, when one does not make the best efforts to understand the other, one wants to convince the other that his/her way of going about things or interpret the world is better. The father does not accept the new, the son does not accept the antiquated way of being of his "old man," and they start focusing on their differences and drift apart from each other. Many times, a parent will try to impose his/her way with more energy than needed and will end up hurting their kids, creating sorrow. The kid will answer back, will be aggressive and will create a vicious spiral of mutual aggressions that many times will end up separating parents from kids for many years, sometimes forever. If they try to understand these differences and accept them (kids forgiving the fact that their parents are just trying to justify their now obsolete way of being, after all they have been as such for almost all their lives; and parents forgiving their kids eager desire to have their own voice in the world, his/her identity, his/her way of seeing things), it will become possible to seal peace between them and be "Agnus Dei" for one another.

In our friendships it is quite common that we face challenging times when we express ourselves impolitely, when we are not there, when a friend needs us most, when we act with indifference to something that is important to them. Or simply act selfishly putting our need to speak ahead of the need to listen. With friends as well, we sometimes focus on differences, giving little opportunity for the relationship to grow and enrich us, since it is through those same differences that we learn new things. It would be a blessing to these relationships, if we could forgive these humanities of ours, of being every now and then egocentric and limited in our ability to understand others. Our friendships also require that we exercise the "Agnus Dei" with others.

Even in our daily routines, when we face that supermarket attendant that is less effective or behaves carelessly about our needs, or that impertinent salesperson that calls us in the most inconvenient moments, or that unknown person that passes by in a hurry and bumps into us, or that careless driver that crosses our path on the highway. All these less pleasant moments of our days usually bring along an undesired surge of adrenaline that, more often than not, pushes us over our limits and leads us to respond and react also in unpleasant manners. If we think for a moment that the supermarket attendant could be in the worst moment of her period agonizing with cramps, that the salesperson has kids to feed, that people in a hurry sometimes actually have a legitimate sense of urgency, we may breathe deeply, take that bad energy away from that unpleasant moment and be "Agnus Dei" as well for these strangers.

As we exercise the "Agnus Dei" concept with our partners in life, our parents, our kids, our friends and even with strangers, we may as well be doing our part in order to create a more peaceful and loving world, renovating our relationships every moment.

However, I believe there are few things that bring us more peace and spiritual redemption than the exercise of self-forgiveness, understanding ourselves as imperfect human beings, capable of making mistakes.

Commonly we play the role of our own judge, condemning our own selves to the eternal fire of guilt, allowing it to reign sovereign in our hearts for all wrong doings of our lives, since we also were teenagers once, and we also made our relationships with our parents something less peaceful. We were also unnecessarily rough with our sons and daughters in a given moment. We have also been indelicate with the loves of our lives, saying heavy words, hurting them and being indifferent to their pain. We also have been, at one moment or another, selfish with our friends, rude to strangers and made mistakes that we never thought we would be capable of.

As we remember these moments, we usually judge ourselves rigidly in our own minds, and consider ourselves guilty for hurting and embarrassing the ones we love and begin to carry heavy chains that weigh on us every single day, many times for the rest of our lives. We will only be able to forgive ourselves and make peace with our own egos, when we begin to understand ourselves as humans, imperfect and incomplete, in a constant state of evolution. We have the power to be our own "Agnus Dei," cutting and throwing away the chains, getting rid of these weights and liberating ourselves to evolve, to grow and move on.

Of course, it will not always be easy since there are circumstances in life where the pain generated is so overwhelming that it will demand from us an inhuman kind of strength to forgive. Please understand that I am not preaching that we ignore aggressions, betrayals, violence, and bad character. A spouse that betrays the other every opportunity he/she gets, a parent that beats his/her kids regularly, an irresponsible driver that takes the life of someone, a person that steals the other, they all deserve the due application of the law, and it would be more than understandable that we would want to get away from these imbalances. Forgiveness shall not serve as an incentive for the mistakes to endure. The spouse that feels constantly betrayed may break ties in order to protect him/herself of future pain and humiliations. Responding to the betrayer with another betrayal will not fix the problem. It would be better if the betrayer is forgiven by his/her loving limitations so chains are not carried on, and he/she may also carry on with his/her life. And this applies to each situation mentioned above. We shall move away from the bad feelings generated by these people. Let the law fulfil its role with the ones at fault while we forgive their imperfections. By doing that, we may go on with our lives in peace. Seeking revenge will only generate more pain. We shall let go and move on. No carrying of chains.

So, I would like to share this message. It is at our reach to incorporate the concept of being Lambs of God, renovating the energies of our relationships, liberating people from their guilt, bringing peace to the ones we love and even to strangers. And just as important, you may forgive and liberate yourself from the mistakes of the past. Learn from the mistakes you've made and evolve, transcend, make peace with your own self and your past, and move on.

We can, and shall be, "Agnus Dei" with others and with ourselves.

THE PIECE OF PAPER THAT CHANGED MY LIFE

"Life is like a box of chocolate. You never know what you gonna get."

From the movie *"Forrest Gump"*

I believe that all of us, at one moment or another, have been dragged into some sort of discussion around the forces that supposedly govern our lives and the potential polarity between fate and self-determination, the antagonism between being a fatalist accepting passively what life brings to us, or being the "owner" of your own destiny, making your own path and being proactive about things.

The fatalists might argue that our fates have already been decided. Life would lead us towards the path we have to follow, we would go through the experiences we have to go and would interact and coexist with the people we must, since it would be through these experiences and interactions that we would learn the spiritual lessons we have to learn, in order to transcend to a new evolutionary stage. This would mean that it doesn't matter how hard you fight to take your life to this or that direction or how much you try to get out of a given state of things, places, people and experiences, life would always lead you back to them, since they would be your spiritual path. Generally passive and self-denied by their beliefs, these people put their destinies in the hands of God and attribute to him their fates. When something good happens, they classify it as bliss and if something bad happens, they attribute such event to the will of God. "That is how God wanted it to be" they say.

Now, in the point of view of the self-determinists, they have the power to govern themselves. For them, nothing would happen by chance. They plan their futures in detail, save money for their vacations, for retirements, make a schedule for their careers and define in which position they want to be by when, and how much money they will be making. They assume a "no excuses" policy and begin to execute their plans. When an adversity beyond their control happens, they call it a "bump in the road" and keep the march, determined as they usually are, until they get to their objectives. These people believe to be making their own destinies and do not attribute to God or luck their successes or the lack of it. If an objective was reached, it was because they planned it well and executed it even better, and therefore, they are winners. If failure occurs, they label themselves as losers, since planning or execution did not go well. Luck was never a factor and God did not get involved in the process.

As I think about these two extreme ways of seeing life and analyze them through the lenses of my own experiences and the experiences of others close to me, I cannot avoid reaching the conclusion that these two approaches are imperfect and limited, since one fails to see how much we can actually make a difference in our fate and the fates of people around us, while the other fails to see God's divine interventions (independently of how you see it), moving pieces around in this giant chess board, changing the game and taking us from one side to the other, so we may go through this or that path and meet (or meet again and again) this or that person.

Throughout my life I have moved from one side to the other a few times, between these extremes. I've had moments when I became passive and self-denying, putting everything on the hands of God, adopting a contemplative approach, seeking indifference about things. If in one side this approach spared me of some frustrations, it also took me to a dead end, with no evolution and a complete disconnection with the world around me. On the other hand, I have already positioned myself as a self-determinist, being the owner of my own destiny and decisions, and needed life to put me back in my place a few times, so I could learn that I do not control all the variables. Bottom line, I needed to go through a normal cycle of learning experiences, so I could reach my own conclusions, that neither one of the extreme approaches actually suited me.

Perhaps the personal experience that best illustrates how these two approaches are incomplete on their own, is the one about an unpretentious piece of paper that changed my life in a definitive way. I believe we all have moments like this in our lives, when a decision that seems to be unimportant, irrelevant really, ends up bringing a fork in the road and defines a path to be followed for the rest of our lives.

It all started when I was at the beginning of my professional career, right after graduating from college in Brazil. After a few months of unemployment, I got a job to work in accounting for an important multinational corporation in São Paulo. After some family celebrations for my first job, I started working, determined to make it a success story.

In light of my total lack of personal and professional preparation (after all I did not study accounting) reality little by little started to show its ugly face, and soon I saw myself being transferred from one department to another, without finding anything that would actually fulfill me. On the other hand, the company itself had a very difficult work environment where things like creativity, initiative and collaboration were not encouraged. Everybody should concentrate on their workstations and behave like little robots, which would suffocate me and would leave me in a total state of frustration. The bosses were dry and indifferent. And to top it off, I fell in love with someone, but was not loved back and became emotionally a mess. I decided that moving to São Paulo and being closer to my job and to the lady I was in love with would make things better. So, to the picture I've just described, we now have to add loneliness and lack of money. Sometimes, I would have for dinner the apple I was saving for breakfast. I did not starve, but almost.

It doesn't take a genius to understand that this was not working. After almost three years swimming against all currents, I figured that my life was taking a much undesired direction and that I was moving quickly towards unhappiness (if I wasn't there already). In a rare moment of bravery, fueled by desperation, for the complete dissatisfaction of my father, I took the hard decision and resigned. I left São Paulo, the apartment, the job, unrequited love, and took an important step in my life. A step back, but important just the same. I went back to my parents' house. To do what specifically, I had no idea. I just knew that the previous alternative no longer suited me.

After months of indecisions, frustrating job interviews and an unsuccessful attempt to go back to academia, I found myself without any money and, at the same time, was asked to help with the house expenses. That was when I took a newspaper ad for English teachers and, even without any previous experience, decided to be brave and showed-up. They took me, and a new and unexpected path opened in front of me. My students loved me, the school started to give me more and more classes to teach, and I found out that I had a talent, until then, dormant inside of me. I could teach. And more importantly, I loved doing it. I would prepare classes with care and dedication. If the class wasn't a total success, I would get frustrated. I was doing that with love and devotion.

I started to make reasonable money, and for the situation I was in at that moment, I was doing ok. It was then that Mr. Destiny came about and decided to turn things upside down. My father was promoted to a position in a small town in the countryside of São Paulo state, 3 hours away. Once again, in a moment of bravery, fueled by desperation, since moving to a small countryside city was not in my plans at that stage of my life, I decided to stay where I was in Campinas. I would not follow them in the moving.

My father went into "panic mode." He came to me and asked: "Son, how do you plan to sustain yourself, all alone, in a big city, as an English teacher?." I hated to admit it, but he was absolutely right. Nevertheless, I went out and found a small apartment, rented it, bought some low cost but good-looking furniture, and moved. I would live alone for the first time in my life.

However, Mr. Destiny wasn't just done yet. Actually, he was just getting started. Moved by his concern of leaving his son behind in a big city, making such limited money and with even more limited perspectives of a better future, my father did not rest until he got me into preparing two résumés that he delivered to two friends from his soccer group. Both friends worked for big multinational companies in the region. Since I was absolutely sure that none of them would bring any results, I carelessly prepared them, and delivered them to my father without signatures (a mandatory practice at the time), since I did not care much about the possible outcomes.

And there it was. All that Mr. Destiny needed to complete his act was there, in his hands, so he could once and for all, turn my life totally upside down.

Three months passed since my parents moved away, and I was already getting used to my new routine (or the lack of it) of an English teacher, making little money but paying my bills. I had already even forgotten about those résumés.

In a nice sunny day, when I got to the English school for my afternoon classes, there was a message for me to call a person at the HR department of IBM. Yes, "the" IBM. I thought to myself: "Could it be???"

I went back home that day with a mix of surprise, apprehension, and excitement. I went to the nearest public phone, since I could not afford to have one in my house (and no, cell phones were not yet a reality back then) and called them. The person on the other side of the line confirmed their interest and scheduled a test and a sequence of interviews. As I hung up the phone, I already knew I was going to be accepted. I felt the winds of change strong inside of me. I just knew that from that moment on, my life would never be the same. Why I felt that way, I can't really tell. I just did. And it was a feeling so strong that did not leave me any doubts. I believe that maybe by then, I had finally learned to "hear" life and its underlying moves. And that day, I heard it loud and clear, saying: _Follow this path, Marcos. Just go this way, now. Go . . .

Two weeks later I was working at IBM, where I had the opportunity to meet some very special people, some of which are still part of my life today. I experienced a fantastic organizational culture and learned things that I still make use of today in my career. But what is most important; I met the woman of my life, with whom I married and had two wonderful kids. The bosses I had there would hire me again in other opportunities and made the bridge for me to be hired by a big company in Miami.

Now, stop and think for a moment on how life can be full of nuances. An unpretentious piece of paper, carelessly prepared, and that was not even signed, changed my life in such a dramatic way for decades and in a sense, is still changing it.

Hadn't I found a dead end in São Paulo, what would have become of my life? If I had succeeded in my other job interviews when I was unemployed, where would I have gone to? If I hadn't ventured myself to become an English teacher, perhaps I would have followed my parents to the small countryside city. What would be of me there? Those résumés, that I must confess were only completed to please my father, would never end up at IBM. If I had refused to make the résumés, what would be of my life as an English teacher? These, and many other questions, will never have an answer.

Some could argue that I made my own destiny, since the decisions I took were the ones who took me along this path. Others could argue that destiny was orchestrating everything all along, taking me to São Paulo, so I could know what I did not want, helping me to discover my talents as an educator, and finally, making use of that piece of paper in order to lead me towards a corporate life that would finally come to fruition, long lasting friendships, my definitive partner in life and self-realization as a father.

Based on the above, I would say that life is a mixture of these two extreme interpretations. We do have to be wise, and often brave, in our decisions. However, I do believe that there is a greater power that orchestrates these comes and goes, being our prerogative to make the best out of each opportunity that comes our way, and of the partners we meet along this journey.

On the polarization between fatalists and self-determinists, my thought is that we shall seek balance among these two forces, always granting opportunities to destiny, so it may give you a hand and open new doors, but we must do our best when they do actually open. Sometimes, destiny will grab you by the hand and will point you in a different direction, not always the one you might think to be the best. It is up to you to accept the direction or not and take the steps towards your own evolution.

Have you stopped to think if something similar ever happened to you? Could it be that you also have a "piece of paper," lost in some forgotten corner of your story, that took you by the hand and led you through a fork in the road, changing dramatically the paths of your life? Think about it.

THE RACE THAT IS WORTH RUNNING

*"Continuous effort—not strength or intelligence—
is the key to unlocking our potential."*

Winston Churchill

Nowadays, everything is about competition. Since we are little, we are impelled to compete in every level of our lives. In the schools, we are taught to be among the best in our classes. In sports, we have to stand out in order to get the attention of coaches and earn the medals and trophies offered in tournaments and events of the like. When we grow up, we have to become number one on this or that to earn a place in the sun, that spacious VP corner office, and the financial compensation that will bring all our dreams (that, more often than we like to admit, are not really ours) to reality.

If we really think about it, in essence there is nothing wrong with competition. It was given the ability to compete, that humans were able to prevail and get to where we are today as species, conquering our temporary sovereignty in this planet (for all the good and the bad that it brings along) and in many cases subjugating all sorts of unfriendly environment existent in the face of the Earth. Used wisely and positively, competition will bring out the best in each of us, in the most varied circumstances.

However, taken to extremes, competition may also bring along what is worst in human beings. Examples of this dark side of competition are abundant, and it may go from a student that cheats in order to get that higher grade or to be approved by a college or university, to the athlete that makes use of illegal substances to reach those tenths of a second or that extra mile that he/she is missing to break a record. Not to mention companies that give a facelift to their financial results in order to reach better appreciation at the stock markets, and executives that cheat and step over colleagues and coworkers in order to get that promotion or raise in salary.

This tendency to compete against everything and everyone is inculcated in our heads and modeled in our behaviors since our early ages (since it is also an essential part of the social economic model that we live in), and we end up replicating this pattern for the rest of our lives, frequently not realizing how it plays a role on making our relationships much more difficult in many levels. It is not unusual that, without noticing, we get involved in "imaginary races" to win over a sibling, the spouse, a school colleague, a coworker, or even a parent or son/daughter. We compete in order to get the attention and approval of our parents, our kids, our teachers, our coaches, the opposite sex, our bosses, of our dearest friends, and if we take these "races" too seriously, we might end up pushing people away, since we begin to see them all as some sort of threat. They could all become competitors at some level, and we could end up failing to build strong connections.

In a world that values high performances and where we are consistently encouraged to become the highest achiever on anything, there will always be people known to us that already ran the New York marathon, read ten books in a month, evolved rapidly in a meteoric career, or lost ten pounds in a week. With this kind of reference around us, it is easy to fall for the temptation of comparing them to our own evolutions that, often, are not as spectacular and we get frustrated. Then, we begin to judge ourselves incompetent and inapt in all fronts of our lives. We end up quitting, stop evolving and fall into a depressive state of stagnation.

As we direct our attention and energy to these external references and run our imaginary races, we miss the point, and forget to focus on what really matters. Our own selves. We miss the opportunity of self-evaluating through a neutral and objective perspective, since we are too busy trying to be better than somebody in something. Better than a hypothetical competitor that represents one of the already mentioned threats, or to have a spectacular performance in something such as this or that person we know has had.

Do we ever question if being better than this or that person is really important? Who are we trying to impress? And we want to be better, why? Does it really matter to be better than someone for the wrong reasons? Will the fact of being better or having more than this or that individual help us become better human beings?

If we stop for a moment to analyze the many aspects of our lives, there is only one competition that really matters. The competition against our own selves. The only comparison that is really worth making is how we are today in comparison to how we were a while ago. The only race that is really worth running is the race against our own selves.

What would happen if we changed our perspectives and began to analyze ourselves with a neutral point of view, without comparing ourselves to others? And what if we adopt the perspectives of the people that really matter to us, how would our performances be as spouses, parents, sons/daughters, or friends? What have we done lately to evolve intellectually or physically? How is our health in comparison to what it was some time ago? How have we evolved in terms of spirituality? How have our contributions evolved in terms of making this planet a better place?

We frequently miss having a more practical and objective approach to evaluate ourselves by a neutral perspective, one that is not affected by this negative competitiveness that surrounds us. I would like to suggest something somewhat unusual, based on an analogy to a management practice.

Those who work in organizations have certainly come across some programs and projects to improve practices and processes, in order to reach higher quality levels of products and services offered to customers. These programs and projects make use of sophisticated methodologies to map processes, identify improvement opportunities, find the root causes of low performances and elaborate action plans that have as main objectives, eliminate such root causes. Nowadays, most of these initiatives are called "Continuous Improvement Programs," that have as source of inspiration the Japanese methodology called Kaizen, created in the post-war world and that was later made popular by Toyota. By this methodology, everything can be improved, and the perspective of the customer is always used to define what is good or bad.

What I would like to suggest is a personal approach to this methodology. I like to call it "Personal Continuous Improvement" and it works similarly to the management program.

The first thing to do is to divide your life into many different aspects. There is the physical you, the intellectual you, the spiritual you, the professional you, there is you as a son/daughter, you as a spouse (or boyfriend/girlfriend), the parent you, the athlete you. Well, there are infinite variants of you. Each of them will deserve individual attention.

Let's take the physical aspect as an example. How is your health today? Have a check-up done and define an initial point of reference. If, as a result of the exam, you find out that you are ten pounds over your ideal weight, and that your cholesterol is a bit high, identify the current practices that are causing unsatisfactory outcomes. Are your eating habits bad? Aren't you exercising regularly? Once you have defined the initial reference and the practices that require improvement, build an action plan. In this situation, you would have to eat healthier and exercise regularly. Do that for a defined period of time. Once that time has passed, have another check-up done, and compare the results. If your weight and cholesterol level improved, don't get satisfied. Remember that the principle here is continuous improvement. Define a new target and go after it.

The same would apply to the intellectual you. How many books have you read in the past six months? What would be the reasons for you reading so little? And could it be that you are always reading about the same topics? What could be getting in the way of your intellectual evolution? Once again, define your initial reference, the improvement opportunities, build a plan to read more and diversify the topics you read about, and implement it. Measure again in six months and make new improvement plans.

The same would also apply to your spiritual side. How far from God are you? And why? What can be done in order to get closer to Him? Once again, we may follow the routine already explained. Initial reference, improvement opportunities, action plan, implementation, reevaluation after some time, new plan.

Now, when we begin to evaluate our performance over the way we interact with other people, we must apply the principle of using their perspective as reference. Every Quality Program has, as primary focus, the requirements of the customers. The same must be applied to your role as a parent, a spouse, son/daughter or as a friend.

Here the evaluation process becomes a bit more complex since it requires being humble, and humble enough and internally strong to listen to candid feedback on how we are performing in these roles. Have you ever thought for a moment that, in our professional lives, we constantly sit down with our customers in order to listen to their opinions about our products and services? However, we do not have the habit of doing the same with the people we love, asking them objectively, how we are performing.

Let's begin with your role as a spouse. From the perspective of your partner in life, how well are you performing this role? What could be done so he/she would feel more satisfied? Have you thought about having this same dialogue with your parents? Or with your kids? Have you actually ever thought about being objectively evaluated by the ones you love? Get ready. You will have to be quite strong and humble to listen to such feedback without being defensive. But once you have turned that corner, you will find yourself with an abundance of material to work on. Your initial reference has been defined, and you will be able to identify your improvement opportunities as a spouse, parent, and any other aspect of your personal life that you select as priority. Build an action plan, implement it, ask for more feedback, check your progress, build another plan and so forth. We can always get better.

After some time repeating this routine, you are likely to enter into a spontaneous personal continuous improvement process. I learned this management methodology way back in my IBM years and started applying it to my personal life since then. I have been doing this for so long, that I have this mechanism almost running in automatic pilot. Once I have been humble enough (usually the hardest part) to identify an improvement opportunity, I immediately start working on it.

Please note that through this approach we haven't compared ourselves to any other person, just with our own selves. We haven't competed with anybody but our own past reference. We haven't raced against anybody but us.

As we shift the focus, moving away from comparisons and from being defensive against imaginary threats, we begin to evaluate ourselves through straight and objective perspectives, without any competitive contamination. We begin to run the race that is really worth running. The race against ourselves. And as we win it, we move at a fast pace towards transforming ourselves into better human beings, and making the world around us healthier, happier, and more harmonious.

Good luck with your Personal Continuous Improvement program.

I want to see you win this race.

THE MIDLIFE OPPORTUNITY

"I want to say now, the opposite of what I said before; I'd rather be this ambulant metamorphosis, than having that old, formed opinion about everything."

Raul Seixas (Brazilian musician and song writer)

After we reach a certain age, the arrival of our birthdays seems to bring along an inevitable retrospective exercise, requesting us to look back and take stock of what took place in the last twelve months, and how our lives have evolved. It is a time of reflections. A time to look at the new wrinkles in the mirror, to realize that the children are a little bigger, that the joints pop a little more often than we would like, and that not everything is as we thought it would be, as we reach such an age.

The truth is that every life phase has its discoveries. I still remember as a child wanting to get to the age of ten. There was some kind of inexplicable magic in reaching a double-digit age. I would certainly feel bigger, more important, more respected. When I got there, I realized that such so desired age brought along its own challenges and responsibilities. Soon after, I wanted to reach fifteen, because I would then be in the fullness of my adolescence.

When I got there, I was greeted by a confused guy, full of hormones that created the biggest physical and emotional mess. But I figured that when I got to eighteen, I could drive and would own the world. It was another illusion. I went to college and didn't quite know what I would find there. It was a time of many personal discoveries and revolutions. But regardless, I always imagined that the next phase would bring interesting experiences. There was always some sort of excitement about getting older.

However, after a certain phase, birthdays begin to bring with them a certain level of discomfort. It seems that deep in our minds we begin an undesirable but inevitable countdown, and blowing out the candles is no longer as stimulating as it used to be. The newly acquired age is no longer so exciting. The time lived begins to charge heavy tolls that we have less and less desire to pay. The feeling is that of wanting to play hide and seek with old age, trying to escape from it as much as possible, but always knowing that sooner or later it will find us, and will announce to us loud and clear that we have been uncovered.

- Ahaaaaa... I got you, Marcos! You thought you were going to fool me, didn't you? Nananana... you can get out from behind the couch... one, two, three...

There's a whole negative myth about getting older. As our body is no longer as attractive, nor as efficient as it once was, and our energy levels are no longer the same, a misperception is created that we are no longer socially as useful as before. Job offers dwindle, doors begin to open less and less, and society expects from us a less creative, less innovative pattern of behavior, without much change. We are impelled to move on by repeating the daily routine: going to work, coming home at the end of the day, watching TV, taking care of the children, kissing our loved ones, going to bed, and repeating it all over again the next day. The path is already mapped out before us, and this is how it has to be for the rest of our lives.

A middle-aged person has his professional and financial demands. You have to worry about staying competitive, saving money for your children's studies, for retirement and, whenever possible, seeking that promotion to improve future prospects. You also have to maintain an already predetermined appearance, with gray hair neatly trimmed, dress respectfully, and be less flamboyant in your behavior. If we want to follow this path, the route is already delineated, the expectations are already outlined, the stereotype is already defined and all we have to do is go ahead, filling in these gaps. But does it have to be that way?

When I reached the so-called middle age, I couldn't help but feel disdain for this perspective. When I stopped and analyzed such a situation, I felt that I was in one of the best phases of my life. I had the realization that I had finally reached a point where I had enough practical knowledge to create new things with propriety and substance. I felt that I had unprecedented conditions to positively impact the company I worked for, and the lives of the people around me. And all this without the youthful arrogance and emptiness of academics, fresh out of school desks, who think they know the truths of life, but do not yet have the scars from the battlefields. I felt in a position to share experiences, lived situations, to illuminate the paths of those who have not yet decided to open their eyes, to show the north to those who still look south, to draw attention to the sounds and flavors that bring indescribable pleasures, to teach the words that open and close doors for those who still ignore their existence. Anyway, I felt that intelligence and knowledge had on their side, the most powerful of allies, which only comes with time and age, and which is called wisdom.

Many call this phase of life the "Midlife Crisis," because it is in it that people realize that they already have less to live than they have already lived. When this fact "sinks in," they start to do things that until then, for various reasons, they had not done yet. They buy that sports car, find a new romance or end unhappy relationships, start doing extreme sports, change their look and often take risks on something in life that, until then, they had not taken. But when we look at this short list, where do you notice the signs of a crisis? A new car, a new love, more daring, new look, taking new risks; When I look at this list I see much more of a scenario of renewal and new possibilities than a crisis. It reminds me of that motto of the business world that says that, in Chinese, the same word that is used to define a crisis is also used to define an opportunity. That's it! I think I fit this definition much better. I believe I have lived through my "Midlife Opportunity."

When I look back at that moment in my life, I feel like I went through the most creative years. I feel like I revolutionized myself once again. I feel like I was (and still am) flourishing. It was only at that age that I resolved to express myself publicly by writing in a way I had never done before; And believe me, this activity did more good things to me than to any of my readers, because it made me have to live what I wrote, to set an example, to walk the path I had suggested myself. Also at this stage, I finally taught my first course on my professional specialty, sharing my knowledge with other professionals and also passing on to them my experiences, sharing the stories of my "scars from the battlefield." A refreshing experience that opened new doors for me and an alternative professional route. Also at that stage, I reached the weight I wanted to be on. I know it's hard to believe, but I'm just as thin as I was when I got married more than two decades ago.

At that time in my life, I had the possibility to innovate in my work like few times in the past and took a role where my experiences were applicable and valued. I had interactions with presidents, vice presidents, general managers, and learned a lot of new things. I took new courses, learned more, evolved more. In addition to all this, I decided to fulfill an old aspiration to change my look to something less square, less welded, less standard. I've always wanted to experience the freedom of letting my hair grow. Some astrologers say that a Sagittarius, being half man half horse, always wants to have a beautiful and long "mane" and I think they are right.

Anyway, at such an age I began a wonderful process of reinventing myself, which is still far from over. I have plans that can take this process of reinvention even further. Really, I feel like I'm still living my "middle-age opportunity," and I hope to keep going, and renewing and reinventing.

This phase of life seems to turn on some engines that have been turned off and propels us in new directions. The impression I have is that I feel the game is already approaching those defining moments, and that there is no longer much time to waste on indecision, or to be wasted on banalities. It's time to produce, create, evolve.

I believe that everyone goes through these phases of transformation sooner or later. Some repress them, others prefer to ride the wave of this renewal. I'm obviously in the second group. But everyone changes, even the repressed, if only a little.

If you are about to enter this phase, are going through it, or have already passed it and feel that you must make good use of your "midlife opportunity," I suggest using these renewing engines to your advantage and creating, changing, renewing. Everyone has a dormant talent that isn't being exploited as it could. Everyone has something more to say to the world, whether it's writing a blog, painting pictures, playing an instrument. Everyone has an activity they'd like to learn to do, whether it's canoeing, rafting, skydiving, or singing in the church choir. And surely you also have your own experiences to share, stories to tell, knowledge that is stored, ready to light the way for the youngest. You also have your scars to share. And if you feel like changing the look, go for it. Reinvent yourself. Don't just think "outside the box," but get out of it literally. We are our own creation. Recreate yourself. Make your midlife crisis turn into an opportunity.

And if you are still young and far from reaching this stage, I hope that this will serve you to better understand this process of renewal, which may be happening to people close to you, such as your parents, uncles, neighbors, friends, and other acquaintances. And remember, one day you'll get there too!

About Passion and Detachment

*"If you change the way you look at things,
the things that you look at, change."*
Wayne Dyer

Nowadays everything seems to be so dynamic and mutable that it feels like we are nearly destined to have short-term relationships, either with the things that are around us or with the people we interact with. There are coworkers or school mates that enter our lives, establish a connection with us, captivate us in one way or another, and soon they are off and gone, in search of a new job opportunity, a new studying option or a new adventure of some sort. At work, new projects are launched, get us excited, mobilize resources and people, change our lives, but when they are finally implemented, a newcomer arrives with some new ideas or the latest management fashion and decides that what was done is no longer so important and everything must be changed, or that something totally different must be created. The same thing happens with objects that we consume. What is now considered the best of the best in terms of technology and design, will be obsolete in a matter of months, and in a short time we see ourselves getting rid of things we once thought were awesome, since they are no longer so interesting.

Since it is human nature to get attached to people, objects and to things that we do or create, we end up suffering with these comes and goes. We are stimulated by all means to be passionate about our work and for the consequent results of our creations, to be enchanted by our material possessions that came out of so many hours of hard work, we feel energized by people that cross our ways either by their internal or external beauty, their ideas, thoughts, and behaviors. But suddenly we see ourselves forced to say farewell to all these creations, acquisitions, conquests, friendships.

We suffer because we have to break away from all sorts of attachments we cultivate. If that car was the best, why did it have to be stolen, or why did I have to have that total loss accident? That is really bad, isn't it? That person I'd created such a connection with had to move to another country. That is terrible . . . right? This project was going so well, and our boss decided to change everything. How foolish. He/she is going to throw everything that was done away. Stupid, isn't it? Well, allow me to offer you quite a different way to look at these losses, which constantly bring us so much undesired emotional pain.

Some time ago I read a fable that I will try to reproduce in a free adaptation, since, once again, I unfortunately did not keep this gem in my files.

Our story says that in a medieval village, a boy around eighteen years of age was walking around the local fair when he was approached by an old man. He was bringing along, tied to a rope, a nice-looking healthy horse, that for many reasons, he could no longer sustain. Afraid that the animal would suffer, he just wanted to donate it to someone who would take good care of him. Our young man swiftly offered himself to take care of the animal, thanked the old man a million times for the unexpected gift, and went home happier than ever with his new acquisition.

As he arrived home, he rushed to tell all the family about his incredible luck. In the middle of hundreds of people, he had been chosen to receive that beautiful animal as a gift. Everybody celebrated excitedly, except his grandfather, known for his wisdom. The boy couldn't help noticing the silence of the old man and asked him; "Aren't you happy grandpa? I got this beautiful animal as a gift. Isn't that awesome?" And to that, the old man answered, "It seems to be my dear grandson. Time will tell." The boy turned away a bit annoyed, called his grandfather crazy, and went celebrate with the others.

For many weeks our young man enjoyed his just acquired animal. He would ride through the fields all inflated as he would pass by the young ladies of the village, feeling the greatest. However, on a nice sunny day as he was riding, the horse stepped in a hidden hole in the ground and tumbled, taking along our young friend in a spectacular fall. Both broke a leg. The animal had to be sacrificed and our friend had to be in bed for a long time. Everybody was devastated, except the grandfather, that didn't seem to be affected. As the boy took notice of his grandfather's apparent indifference, he asked; "Don't you see that now I no longer have my horse and I am destined to stay in bed for weeks? This is terrible." And the old man replied, "It seems to be my grandson, but only time will tell." Once again, our boy got upset. He even felt offended by his grandfather's reaction and told him to leave the room. The old man walked out in silence, without a change of expression and went back to his duties.

A few weeks had passed since the accident when a war against a neighbor country exploded, and the authorities went door to door recruiting young men to be sent to the battlefield, giving preference to the healthy ones, and most importantly, to the ones who had a horse to mount. For obvious reasons, when they got to the house of our young friend, he was dismissed from military services, since he did not gather the necessary physical conditions nor had an animal to mount. As the authorities left the house, everybody was relieved and thanked God for the incredible luck our young friend had for being dismissed from what appeared to be a terrible fate. He then called his grandfather, apologized, and said he was right, since he had escaped war and that was very good. Once again, with an unchanged face, the grandfather accepted the apologies and said, "It seems to be my grandson, but only time will tell." The boy lowered his head, feeling bad for the evident lack of mental health of his grandfather and avoided arguing this time.

It happened then, that the war did not last but a few months. The country of our friend walked out in victory and the soldiers that fought came back home covered in glory. Many young men of the village that had a similar age of our injured friend became heroes from one day to another, had their names listed in a public monument, and began to receive lifelong benefits. As our young man got out of bed, he saw himself diminished beyond his friends, was perceived as a loser, and had to go back to work while the others enjoyed the benefits offered by the government to the war veterans of his age. At home, everybody thought him to be very unfortunate. Feeling depressed, he went to speak with his grandpa who seemed to be the only one who did not look at him in a different way, and once again heard from him that the situation could appear to be unfortunate now, but only time could really tell.

Flowers on the Balcony

After a few years, that same neighbor country that had fallen in defeat was now much stronger and mercilessly invaded the country of our friends, took the capital, and controlled everything. Moved by a spirit of revenge and shame for the previous humiliation, they searched for every soldier that had fought in the old war and had become heroes and executed them one by one. Since our friend did not fight that war and therefore did not have his name listed in a public monument, he was spared this terrible fate and once again exalted his great fortune. But as he remembered his wise grandfather, that by now had already passed, and thought of his usual passivity, he understood that it was better to wait, so he could better interpret if that was in fact good or not.

It happened then, that the invaders needed workers and all the men that were not executed were forced to work as slaves to their new sovereigns, and our friend who, at this stage, was not so young anymore, saw himself forced to work dawn to dusk in construction, plantations, food storage, transportation, and all sorts of activities. However, our friend had already learned to see things in a dynamic way and did not lament over his apparent lack of fortune this time.

After years of forced work in many different functions, he had learned a bit of everything. The invaders that were now facing a civil war, decided to leave, and left behind a devastated country. Since our friend had become a man of many talents and had learned a lot from his grandfather, he became a respected figure and was chosen to become the new leader of his small village. Evidently, at this point of his life, he no longer judged that to be good or bad. He had already learned by then, that only time would really tell.

This little story, that in part was originated in what I read years ago and in part was a creation of my own imagination, serves to illustrate what happens in our lives and suggests that we shall ponder before we celebrate or suffer intensely, over what in a given moment, we understand to be extremely good or tragically bad.

If you receive a promotion, go on and celebrate, but stay put, since a year from now your whole department could be discontinued. However, if that happens, don't cry a river, since you may get an even better job, thanks to the experience acquired in the previous position. If you bought a new car, enjoy your new acquisition, but keep in perspective that one day it will get old, or it could be stolen, or it could be the victim of an accident that would result in a total loss. Don't lament so much if that happens, since this might be just the opportunity you needed to acquire an updated version or a more economic model. If a person has captivated you for whatever reason, make the best out of this relationship, but keep in perspective that one day this person will go in search of new horizons, new challenges, new experiences. And if that happens, don't grieve so much over this loss, since this change might result in growth for the one who left and will open a space for a new friendship to grow in your life. If you just won a prize in your workplace for a project or job well done, celebrate and live this moment with pride, but keep in perspective that the work environment changes, new priorities arise and in a short period of time, the work you've done will no longer be as relevant, and something else will take its place. But even if that happens, don't be sorry since novelties will bring along new opportunities to shine.

In summary, we shall always raise the awareness that only time will respond if something is good or bad, since only the development of the facts and the passing of the years will tell, when we look back and see things in perspective, and are able to connect the dots between the many events that took place. Only then we will be able to see the whole thing as a film, scene after scene, telling the whole story. If we look only to photographs of events, isolated in their own time, we may easily elude ourselves and rush to precipitated conclusions.

We surely must be passionate about our new projects, material acquisitions, new friends, and partners of journey, after all, this is what adds flavors to our lives. However, we shall always keep in perspective that life changes and that things, jobs, and people come and go. We shall develop on a daily basis a sense of detachment and learn to say goodbye, allowing life to flow on its natural course, evolving with each experience, and carrying along the best of everything that crosses our ways.

Live with intensity each season. But keep in mind that every winter is succeeded by spring, and each summer brings autumn as it ends.

THE POWER OF PERSEVERANCE
SHINE AND LET SHINE

"I've failed over and over and over again in my life and that is why I succeeded."

Michael Jordan

Let's imagine for a moment that you are a basketball coach in need of an experienced player to complete your team. Then you get a call from this guy that says he is not as tall as some other players (he is "just" 6,6), and that fact alone does not impress you very much to begin with. Then he goes on saying: "When I was a teenager, I was rejected by my varsity school team. As a professional, I missed more than nine thousand shots, I lost around three hundred games and in ten percent of those, I was responsible for the final shot for the tie or for the win and . . . missed. In my first five seasons, I didn't win a thing, and missed almost a whole year because of an injury." Of course, after this brief introduction, you are about to dismiss the "shorty." But then you allow him one last sentence, and he says: "When I was finally accepted in the school team, I was appointed as one of the best in the nation and got a scholarship for one of the biggest universities in the country, where I came to be the national champion, making the final shot that would untie the game in the last second. As a professional I was national champion six times, scored the most points in the league for ten years and was Olympic champion twice." And then you realize you were about to dismiss nothing less than Michael Jordan.

Now let's change sports. Pretend you are in search of a Right Back for your weekend soccer team, and someone recommends you this guy who was rejected nothing less than fourteen times, before he finally had a shot in a professional team. The first thought that comes to your mind is, why in the world would I give a chance to someone who was rejected so many times? Well, you would give him this chance because after so many rejections, this skinny and clumsy guy would become world champion five times, three times playing for his club and twice for his national team, would appear in four world cups, would become the only player in the history of the game to play in three consecutive world cup finals and would be the record keeper of the number of times someone played for the Brazilian national team. Yes, you would be giving Cafú his fifteenth rejection.

But let's leave the sports arena for a moment and talk about music. You are now looking for a rock'n'roll band to animate a graduation party, and you get this suggestion of hiring this band that, in their first attempt to record an album, was rejected by the record company because their style sounded outdated. Would you hire them? Well, you would, because after digging a little deeper you would find out that the rejected band is the one that sold the most albums in music history, and the band members, some guys named John, Paul, George, and Ringo, are in the list of the most influential people of the twentieth century.

Now, in search of someone to write you a story, you get the references of a gentleman who was fired from the newspaper he worked for when he was young, since they thought him to lack imagination and creativity. So why would you hire him? Because this gentleman would later become the founder of the greatest amusement park in the world and would create dozens of characters that today are part of our culture. The corporation that takes his name, Walt Disney, has been selling dreams to the world for generations.

And if by any chance you are looking for someone to lead a major project or an organization, I may suggest the name of this gentleman that brings in his résumé two bankruptcies and that was defeated in eight elections. Why would you hire him as a leader? I just forgot to mention that after all that, he became President of the United States and, thanks to his leadership, the country did not get divided in two during the civil war. Today he is considered one of the greatest leaders of all time. Of course, I am talking about Abraham Lincoln.

Now try to imagine just for a second if Michael Jordan had given up basketball when he was rejected by his school team. Or if after missing so many shots, he would come to believe that he wasn't good enough. Or that after getting hurt at the beginning of his professional carrier, he wouldn't have persevered to go back and play again. Basketball would have lost maybe its greatest star of all times.

And what if Cafú had given up trying after his fourteenth rejection? If he hadn't persevered just once more? We Brazilians would have lost our captain, World Cup champion in 2002 and most likely the history of soccer could have been different.

And imagine if the Beatles had given up after they were rejected by the first record company they tried out. Or if they hadn't accepted the invitations to play for months and months in Hamburg, Germany, where no one knew them before they conquered a place in the sun? Many bands remained anonymous because they did not persevere and did not fight for their dreams. Without the Beatles the history of music and pop culture would have been different.

And think for a moment if Walt Disney had taken seriously what he was told about not having imagination or creativity. The world would have lost one of its greatest creative minds.

However, we would have had much more serious implications if Abraham Lincoln had given up his political career when he lost his eighth election and wouldn't have persevered one last time. The history of the world would have been different, since the USA as we know it today, probably wouldn't exist.

Examples as these ones are abundant in the media and literature throughout history. And what do they have in common? They all failed miserably and were rejected many times, but persevered, kept trying, and did not give up in the first denial. Nor in the second. Not even on the third. For many times, they had to play in secondary teams, or in places with no expression whatsoever, work in places where they could not shine, but they went on. What made these cases such success stories was one common thing called perseverance. It's the fact that they brought inside them a dream they were chasing and no matter what they were told by others, the many defeats they had, and the negatives they received, they kept on trying until they got what they wanted. A place to shine.

Doesn't this make you wonder how many times in our lives we came across adversities, and ended up giving up on our dreams or ideas, when everything we needed was to try again just one more time? The problem is that we

Flowers on the Balcony

never know for sure when the time will come for us to hear a yes, and it could be that it is just waiting, hidden behind our next attempt.

The fact is that in life, we will hear more "nos" than "yesses." There is always someone ready to say we will not make it, that what we are doing is not worth the effort, that our ideas do not make any sense, or that we should stop inventing novelties and just do what everybody else does. The world around us is always ready to discourage every daring or innovative step that we consider taking. And these are precisely the moments that we must search for our inner strength, to carry ourselves one more step ahead, to persevere for one more day, to keep trying once more, until one day we hear a yes. And if we are lucky to have someone on our side that will encourage us, that will provide reassurance, that will push us further, even better, as the case of Cafú and his wife Regina, who was there for him after each rejection he received.

But most people around us carry the weight of their own denials, their own frustrations, their own surrenders. That is why when they see someone shining or trying something new, their first reaction will most likely be negative. As we receive this type of criticism, these words of discouragement, these "nos," we feel our fears and insecurities rise and turn into giants. In these moments we need to be strong, look our fears and insecurities in the eye, and not lay our arms down. Our next attempt could bring a different result, and we could come across someone in search of innovation, thoughts, and ideas just like ours.

The society we live in is conditioned to focus first on the negative, on what we did wrong, on what didn't work right. We end up following that pattern, focusing on our own failures, and losing sight of the good things we did. If we only look at the shots we missed at the buzzer, or the rejection received in a job interview, on the prize that we did not win, on the idea that was not supported by others, on that presentation that your boss disliked and asked you to change from start to finish, we will certainly feel as the last of the human beings on earth, and will feel discouraged to continue trying to make another final shot at the buzzer, to go out and try another job interview, to be creative and try something new, and to try walking on paths never trailed before. And the world might end up losing the genius we all carry within, who is just waiting for a chance to shine.

Now, what if we look at this matter from a different perspective? How many times in our lives have we ended up playing the role of the negative agent? How many times have we discouraged the new, the different, the last second shot of someone, maybe with one of our employees, friends, spouses, kids? Have you thought about the number of times you had the opportunity in your life to help someone to change things around and become a Cafú? Our world is full of rejected individuals, people that hide in the shadows, or that gave up trying on their will to shine, given the "nos" received since their early ages, from negative and limiting parents, or since the beginning of the school lives, with teachers that would repress the genius that each child brings within. Our roles as leaders in our organizations, schools, communities, and mainly in our families, is to break the chain of "nos" and make flourish the "yesses" and stimulate the rise and development of new Michael Jordans, Walt Disneys and Lincolns. Yes, we have this power, through words of motivation, candid and well-intended feedback, encouragement, and acceptance. We all have the power to be as Regina, Cafú's wife.

Let's raise awareness about our roles on both sides of this story. In other words, how frequently we refrain from providing that word of motivation or encouragement to someone who just received a no in life, or even on the number of times we were the bearer of the denial. Couldn't we have had a different approach?

However, the most important thing is to be inspired by examples such as Michael Jordan, Cafú, Lincoln and many others that would be worth mentioning, and keep trying, until we finally get our chance to shine. And the world will then know the beauty and genius that we bring within.

May you shine and help others shine.

TAKING GOOD CARE OF OUR LOVE TRIANGLES

"A relationship shall serve for both to feel supported in their unrests, to teach mutual trust and respect for the differences that exist among them..."
Drauzio Varella

As our children grow, their behaviors are remodeled, their priorities are revised, and as a result of these changes, our concerns and attentions as parents also have to change. As they begin to look at the opposite sex with less childish eyes, and feelings and emotions begin to manifest, a new universe of possibilities, risks, and opportunities present themselves, and begin to demand from us, parents, a different level of guidance and counseling. And as an old saying suggests; "Matters of the heart; proceed with caution."

Few things challenge us more as human beings than understanding the opposite sex, its nuances, its emotions, its ways of thinking about the world, its reactions, its urges, its pains, its fears, its way of loving. If for us adults, dealing with this complexity represents a tremendous challenge, then imagine for a preteen, who is still discovering the world.

When my kids went into puberty, I wanted to sit down with them and give a kind of lecture, like a coach does before an important game. Tell them: "Hey, look, be careful what you say, remember to always show attention, do this and don't do that, affection is always good, in moments of tension, take it easy..." and millions of other tips. However, as I did this mental exercise, I imagined them with wide eyes and jaws dropped at such complexity. Then I remembered that, the more important and difficult the coach said the game would be, the more anxious and nervous I would become. Assuming that it would only frighten them and perhaps even temporarily scare them away from such a tremendous challenge, I abandoned the idea of a tactical lecture and resolved to deal with the matter differently, as the need presented itself. More subtle; perhaps more effective, but no less challenging.

But seriously, the truth is that understanding the opposite sex is a mix of art and science, and there is a lot of good literature about it. One that always comes to mind and that I recommend reading at any stage of life or type of relationship involving the opposite sex is "Men are from Mars, Women are from Venus." In this book, the author (John Gray) makes use of an amusing analogy to develop the subject of our differences and how best to understand and manage them, making our coexistence with people of the other sex something even more pleasant and less susceptible to conflicts and disagreements. He creates the fiction that men and women came from different planets, men, from Mars, and women from Venus, and that for some reason, both were forced to abandon their home planet and came to cohabit Earth.

So far so good. The problem was that both brought from their home planets their habits, values, chemistry, opinions, and ways of seeing life, and then the conflicts began. Martians thought that Venusians would like the things they liked, would do things that Martians did, and would feel the feelings that Martians felt. So did the Venusians about their new Martian friends, thinking they would communicate in the same way as they did, and that they would enjoy the world as they did. When both Martians and Venusians realized the abyss that existed between them, they became frustrated and disappointed. However, as they were hopelessly attracted to each other, they had no other solution than to seek mutual understanding, and the first step to make this possible was to accept the fact that they were different.

I believe here lies the key that opens the door to all the possibilities of mutual understanding between men and women. The acceptance of the fact that we are different. I think this is one of the few situations in which being empathetic has a slightly limited reach, since, by doing the exercise of putting ourselves in the other person's shoes to see the world from their point of view, and try to feel their pains, understand their anxieties, fears and thoughts, in the vast majority of cases we will carry with us the legacy of being male or female. It will always be challenging, a man to put himself in the place of a woman to try to understand her better and vice versa, since we will almost always look at problems and situations from a male or female idiosyncrasy. How can a man feel to perfection what a woman feels in a given situation, without the reference of previously being a woman? And how can a woman think like a man, without having lived as one before?

Among the most striking and interesting differences that we have to manage on a daily basis is the fact that men are, most of the time, seeking to fix the most diverse situations with a relentless practicality. From the moment someone begins to describe a problem to us men, immediately our head begins to articulate the possible solutions, and we begin to search for the best way to apply them. But when women are sharing their problems, they are, for the most part, just seeking understanding and validation. They just want to hear that their pains and anxieties are legitimate. When we, men, begin to offer solutions and seek to solve in the most practical way possible, the problems exposed by a woman, we feel we are the best, since we are fixing everything. Right? Big mistake. When we do this, we are actually decreasing the size of the problem, and by doing so, we are invalidating what women are feeling. With this, we are only frustrating their desire to be cherished and comforted. In other words, while they want a hug, we end the conversation and turn our backs, leaving them alone, with solutions that they could have created themselves, and thinking that we are the greatest. When they express their frustration, we get frustrated too, thinking that our effort to solve the problems was not properly appreciated. It's just that back on Mars it was like that, John Gray would say. There, we fixed everything in a practical and objective way. On Venus, women supported and comforted each other before solving problems.

Another thing that commonly distances men and women is the way they communicate, or silence, and how what is communicated or silenced is interpreted. While women prefer to express their feelings and frustrations, as a rule using superlatives like "never," "always," "nobody," "everybody," to emphasize their point of view, men, on the other hand, enter their silent "thinking caves." So, when a woman says, "No one ever notices the things I do," the man tends to respond with a negative by saying something like, "Don't be so dramatic, when you implemented that project that time, people did notice." Of course, this answer will only make it worse. In fact, what the woman is saying in masculine language is, "I'm feeling ignored by you right now, and I would love it if you could make me feel more important and give me a compliment or give me a hug." Men, on the other hand, when they are going through a moment of stress or doubt, tend to silence and get into a thinking vicious circle, seeking practical solutions to their problems. By noticing the silence of their partners, women commonly interpret that they might be the problem, and think that they have done something wrong or that they are being deliberately ignored. When they try to "get into the cave" to understand what's going on, they're seen as trespassers, and there we have the ingredients for another unnecessary discussion.

I remember once reading in a scientific research magazine, the theory that most women would use more the right side of the brain and men, as a rule, more the left side. This would mean that most women tend to have a more emotional and creative approach to day-to-day situations, but on the other hand, they would not have the same skills in terms of time management. Most men would be more practical; however, they would have limited ability to deal with aesthetics and a questionable taste for decorations, matching colors, and styles.

An example of this would be how, in general, men and women get ready to go out. While most men behave like a Ferrari mechanic changing a tire during a race, getting ready in 5.7 seconds, without much concern if that green shirt matches those brown pants, women position themselves in front of a mirror and start working on a work of art. As a consequence, only the right side of the brain will be stimulated, causing any perception of the passage of time to be totally ignored. And here comes the car racing mechanic to put some pressure in order to accelerate the creative process. Have you ever tried to paint a picture or make a sculpture with someone next to you saying:

"Come on, you are going to get us late, we should be on our way, this is impossible, why do you have to paint it so much? And why do you have to worry about choosing what material to use?"

You wouldn't like that, right? That is how they feel when rushed to finish their work of art. And the worst part is that, when the art is done, most men are actually worried about getting in the car and leave, not even noticing the results of such careful work. It's like someone would say, "Put your painting back in the trunk and get in the car so we may leave at once. We are very late." How frustrating would that be for an artist?

I could spend hours talking about the possible and hypothetical differences that exist between men and women, but we need to remember that, for each rule, there are many exceptions, and not every man or woman will fit the examples mentioned. But the point here is to draw attention to the fact that herein lies the secret to success in any relationship. Accept the fact that differences exist and learn to understand and manage them.

And when I say that this concept applies to any relationship, I mean that, regardless of whether the couple is made of a man and a woman, or if it is made of any variation or sexual orientation between two human beings, managing differences and reconciling diversities, whether of cultural, spiritual, or philosophical origin, is of fundamental importance to the success of any loving union.

If we let these differences grow larger and get in the middle of two people who love each other, such differences can gradually weaken the relationship, and make each person become defensive about their own way of being, leading each one to focus on themselves, and the connection between them will be lost little by little.

If I could give my children just one piece of advice for their future love life, it would be that in a relationship it is necessary to take care of the three people involved. You might be wondering, "Three people? What do you mean, three people?" Yes, there are three people to be cared for in a relationship. The "I," the "You" (in this case, the other person) and the "We." As we get involved in a relationship, it becomes the third person involved, and it will deserve as much or more attention as the other two. If we prioritize only the "I" or the "You," this relationship (the "We") is doomed to failure. It is very difficult for us to understand this reality.

We can't just think about the "I," trying to make the other person change and adapt to our world and our reality. We have to consider the other person, understand their world, their origins, their legacies, their fears, their dreams, and their needs. That person didn't just materialize in front of you. It brings a whole story, a whole life of emotions, traumas, values, memories, aspirations, that now, whether we accept it or not, have become part of the "We." As many of us read in Antoine de Saint-Exupéry's book "The Little Prince," we are forever responsible for what we have tamed.

However, neither should we focus only on the "You" (the other person), annulling your own self and not shining your own light. If we don't love and respect ourselves, the chances of someone else loving and respecting us are drastically reduced. Believe me, for I am speaking from experiences, lived in relationships from a distant past.

Finally, there is the "We," this ethereal and bodyless being, but who is as present as the other two people. If we do not take good care of the "We," feeding it, nurturing it, cherishing it every day, most likely the relationship will be just navigating between the "I" and the "You." Little by little the "We" will find itself suffocated and dying. The death certificate will state as cause of death, "Chronic Malnutrition."

Every relationship must be treated as a love triangle where the three vertices, the "I," the "You," and the "We," should feel happy and loved. If only one of the vertices of this love triangle is happy, something is wrong.

I would like to leave this reflection on how we deal with our differences with the people around us and, especially, with the people we love the most. Do we recognize the fact that there is a "We" to be cared for and managed? Are we properly taking care of every corner of our love triangle? Let us try to identify, recognize, and understand these differences and make the "We" the most important person in our life as a couple. The strongest vertex of our triangles. Only then, we will seal the peace between Mars and Venus (or any other planet that represents you).

DON'T BECOME A GARBAGE TRUCK

"Like Sandalwood, Perfume the Axe That Falls on Them."

Buda

Unlike many people, one of the things I enjoy the most is to receive positive messages and thoughts by email or social media. Despite the difficulty of finding time to read them with the necessary attention, I always keep them in a separate folder for a later review, when daily commitments allow me. Most of the time I am able to find something that is worth reading, in the midst of poor jokes and chains that do not aggregate much. Every now and then, I end up finding a true gem that makes me think and reflect about my own attitudes and serves as a source of inspiration for me to improve my own approach to life.

Some time ago, I received quite an interesting little story that well exemplifies what happens to us in our day to day, as we interact with people around us. It's called "The Law of the Garbage Trucks" and as in previous occasions, I reproduce here in free adaptation.

The story is about an executive, that had just arrived at his destination after a long flight and took a taxi in order to get to his hotel. The taxi driver, after receiving his instructions and the hotel address, began his journey calmly, with no rush, when he was abruptly cut off by another car, and only for a miracle, was able to avoid the collision. The driver of the other car, ignoring the fact that he was the one at fault, still had the nerve to open the window and scream all sorts of offenses to the taxi driver. To the executive's complete disbelief, the taxi driver reacted in a very balanced manner, made a "thumbs up" sign to the reckless driver, smiled and continued on his path, without complaining or returning the offenses received.

The executive was amazed with that situation. He was used to reacting strongly to each occasion, never allowing a defying or offensive attitude to go by without a response in the same tone. Filled with indignation over that passive reaction, he decided to question the taxi driver and said:

"My "friend," that idiot almost sent us to the hospital. He almost destroyed your car. You were driving in your lane, under the speed limit. You were doing everything as you were supposed to. How could you accept that he would still offend you without giving any response? Why did you allow yourself to be offended without any reaction?"

The taxi driver once again smiled, looked at the review mirror so he could see the executive's reaction and answered:

"Because he was a garbage truck 'sir.'"

Confused with the answer, the executive looked ahead and tried to find the other car, that at this time, had already left in a different direction. He was positive though, that it was not a garbage truck. Laughing about the expected reaction, the taxi driver explained:

"I am not talking about the car, but about the driver. He was indeed the real garbage truck. And like him, there are lots of people out there moving around carrying a lot of garbage, full of frustrations, traumas, disappointments. They eat badly, they drink what they shouldn't, watch TV shows that broadcast hate, envy, and other bad stuff. They take along with them all the garbage from other people and from the world around them, accepting and responding to all sorts of defiance and insult. As they do that, they turn themselves into loaded garbage trucks, looking for a situation, place, or person to unload upon. This one, for example, was dying to unload all his garbage over me, but I did not grant him permission to do so. If I had allowed him to unload it on me, I would have spoiled the rest of my day and would have become the one in the hunt for another poor soul to unload my own garbage over. Many times, we end up unloading all this garbage at home, over the people we love the most, like our wife, our kids, or even over our friends. And they have nothing to do with it."

At this point the executive was already mind traveling, thinking about his boss, who was always in a terrible mood, and the innumerous times he got home grumpy and irritated, short of patience with his own family.

And the taxi driver went on:

"Sir, there are lots of people with so much garbage within themselves that it could even be dangerous to react to them. Imagine if that guy had a gun in his car and I had reacted to his insults. What could possibly happen?"

Once again, the executive had to agree, since he immediately remembered many cases of traffic-related discussions that did not come to a happy ending. The taxi driver finalized his line of thought saying:

"What happens Sir, is that we end up taking everything as personal, you know? "Oh, he cut me off," "he offended me," thinking that the whole problem is about us. In fact, the whole problem is about him. He is the one loaded with bad stuff and is trying to unload it at the first opportunity. If you allow me a piece of advice Sir, whenever that happens to you, take a deep breath, keep your cool, remember that this has nothing to do with you, it's the other person's problem, and move on. Let the garbage truck pass by, taking away with him all the bad stuff he is carrying. By doing that, you will not allow him to unload on you and you will not take the garbage on to other people, especially the ones you love the most. Do not allow these wandering garbage trucks to spoil your day and the day of other people too. You know Sir, life is too short. It is not worth spoiling it, living like a garbage truck. In the end I pity him, you know? I even pray for him and wish he will be able to find peace."

The taxi driver kept talking about the innumerous "garbage truck" cases that had crossed his path one way or another, but the executive wasn't listening to him anymore. That small example of wisdom had carried him away and made him think about his own approach to similar situations. He thought about his aggressive behavior and the idea of not taking offense from anybody. He remembered the innumerous times he had taken home somebody else's garbage, ruining many nights with his family, arguing about futilities with his wife, being impatient with his kids, and even with himself, smoking an extra cigarette or drinking those "two fingers" of whisky so he could relax, just increasing the amount of garbage he was throwing within his own self.

The executive felt guilty for a moment, for all his behaviors. Trying to move away from that uncomfortable feeling, he reached out for a magazine that was there on the back seat of the taxi and opened it randomly. As he looked at the title of the article he intended to read, he felt a shiver down his spine, and realized he would not get away from some deep reflections so easily. It read: "You cannot control what life brings to you, but you can control the way you react to it."

The executive put down the magazine and started thinking about his life, and how he needed to improve the way he reacted to the world around him. When he least expected, he realized the taxi was already parked in front of his hotel. He paid the taxi driver with a generous tip and thanked him for the useful lessons.

That day he had decided to start a process of change and would work on not taking with him the garbage of others. And what is most important, he decided that he would no longer be a "garbage truck" himself, to anybody. Especially to his family.

As we reflect about this simple example of popular wisdom, it is impossible not to think about famous quotes such as "don't do to others what you don't want others to do to you," "you get what you give" or "what goes around comes around." The fact is what you get from life, is a reflection of what you give to it. If we give love, patience, understanding and smiles, we are sure to receive all of this back. But instead, if we give hate, aggravation, intolerance, angry faces, that is precisely what we will get back in the same intensity or worse.

However, there will always be "garbage trucks" out there, that will bring to us their bad attitudes and messages, independent of anything. It is mostly with these unhappy individuals (and that is precisely what they are) that we need to be stronger in our purpose, in order to block their low vibe energy, not allowing it to be contagious. We have to keep our center and break the chain of such bad energy, since passing that garbage ahead does not make the world a better place at all. We have to build a new daily hygiene habit of cleaning ourselves internally. The same way we take our daily showers washing our bodies on the outside, we have to reflect about our internal filths and clean them out. We have to think about those bad feelings and thoughts that we sometimes cultivate, intentionally or unintentionally, that transform us into emotional garbage cans. This same emotional garbage is many times responsible for health unbalances and diseases that lead us to suffering and physical pain.

We shall also build a better awareness of what we grant permission to come inside our bodies and minds. There is a lot of garbage on TV, internet, videogames, movies, and all kinds of media.

It is also worth watching what we eat and most importantly, the consumption in excess of alcohol and the use of drugs that are so harmful to us. If we allow all this garbage to get into our minds and bodies, it is almost inevitable that we will pass it along to others.

In summary, the suggestion is that we work hard in order to stop these negative chains. Let's be the link where they are discontinued. Let's not pass along the garbage from others and let's work on cleaning our own emotional garbage. Think about it. The alternative is to become a garbage truck. And I don't think you want that for you. Do you?

THE DA VINCI COMPLEX

"Being the richest man in the cemetery doesn't matter to me. Going to bed at night saying we've done something wonderful, that's what matters to me."

Steve Jobs

In modern days society we are born, raised, and educated to live under the concept of specialization. Since we are little, we are questioned by our parents, grandparents, relatives, teachers and by any other curious enough adult, about what we are going to be when we grow up. Or if we want to put this questioning in a perspective that is a bit more serious, what people are really asking is "who" we are going to be when we grow up.

Lawyer, doctor, dentist, engineer, administrator, artist, athlete, the alternatives are countless, and many times we see ourselves face-to-face with a decision-making moment that we are not even close to being prepared for. And unfortunately, this decision-making time is coming earlier and earlier in the lives of our teenagers, that are yet to develop the necessary maturity, or lack the appropriate guidance to face such moment.

The fact is that it comes a time in our lives when we have to make some choices. We have to choose a social role. We have to decide how we are going to add value to our society. We have to define how we are going to make our living and pay our way. However, more often than ideal, we look at this decision, which in most instances will follow us for the rest of our lives, through some distorted lenses. We are instigated by the materialist environment we live in, to guide our choices towards the paths that will lead us to earn more money. We are stimulated to discover the careers or social roles we may perform so we may enrich ourselves as much as possible, rarely asking ourselves how we could possibly do something that would contribute and add more value to the society we live in.

Nonetheless, what bothers me the most with this choice, is not the dry and selfish angle we tend to approach it, but the fact that, the majority of times, this will become an exclusive choice.

Putting it in different words, we are covertly forced to leave behind other abilities, skills, and potentials, to dedicate ourselves to one talent, vocation or simply to exercise a specific career. Since this decision is most of the time guided by financial priorities and not necessarily by the talents and abilities that a person might have, it is not uncommon that we find many people frustrated with their own choices.

It is a shame to see people leaving behind their talents and abilities, that many times are innate or have been developed through years of practice during infancy, to pursue a unique and exclusive activity, since that is what is expected of him/her; total focus in one specialty.

Many times, we are forced to leave behind an artistic talent like playing an instrument, writing, paint pictures, build sculptures, or abilities such as teaching, run marathons, be a good listener, simply because we dedicate ourselves exhaustively to a career that we are under the obligation to make it a success. How many people with a talent to teach have never found their way into a classroom because they have to make money in a different activity that brings higher earnings? With such a need of specialization guided by materialistic objectives, we end up leaving behind a constellation of stars that never had the opportunity to shine.

Another collateral damage of the exacerbated specialization is the fact that our days become a repetitive sequence of actions and we get ourselves into disinteresting routines.

We wake-up every day at the same time, we have the same breakfast, we leave home at the same time, we get the same way to work, we work in the same stuff we worked on the day before, we meet the same people, have lunch with the same group and speak about the same subjects, go back home more or less at the same time through the same highway, have dinner at the same time as yesterday, watch the same TV shows and go to bed finishing a day that was very similar to the day we had yesterday.

Evidently, we become desperate for the weekend or holidays and vacations, so we may get out of this routine that makes us prisoners of monotony. This reminds me of a movie called Groundhog Day, where the main character finds himself stuck in time, waking up every day in the same day, and the only way to break the spell was to connect with the people around him and their emotions. But if that did not happen, he would wake up every day on the same day, would always meet the same people at the same time in the same places to do the same things. Sounds familiar?

I get fascinated by historic figures that today are classified as "geniuses," who added value to the society they lived in, acting in many different fronts of work, many times having very little to do with each other. The most notorious example that comes to my mind is Leonardo da Vinci.

It is said that this gentleman, who was born in the Renaissance around 1450, worked as an inventor, sculptor, painter, mathematician, astronomer, among other activities, always leaving his genius mark in all he did. Some of his ideas and creations were simply way too innovative for his time and only materialized centuries later.

An example like this fills me with inspiration and makes me question this specialization slavery we live in nowadays, and makes me wonder, does it really have to be this way?

Lately, I've been trying to break these handcuffs, allowing myself to dare walking along different paths that before I would not find the time, not opening the door for the opportunities that showed up. I used to resign myself to the fact that I had a job in a company and that was the occupation of my life.

The rare moments I would take the opportunity to do things that really moved me, such as teaching or writing, I would live it thoroughly and would suck the juice out of the "fruit" to the last drop. But it was never enough. Actually, it would always leave a sweet taste in my mouth, making me feel like I needed more, what was typically followed by a feeling of emptiness, as if different potentials that I brought within were screaming for more space, which would be consistently denied.

Today, although I still keep my job in a corporation, I find the time to write, teach, do volunteer work, do some coaching, among other things. This essay, for instance, was written while I was waiting to be seen in a doctor's office and during a flight to Mexico. This time that usually would be wasted, I used to exercise my creativity and express myself. With this change in my behavior, I feel I have a voice in the world. I may express myself and exercise my creativity in a way that previously was impossible.

Couldn't we develop and cultivate a sort of Da Vinci Complex in which, instead of using our free time to watch TV, or waste our waiting time in doctor offices, airports, flights, we use it to exercise our dormant talents, which in many cases were given to us by divine intervention, and are forgotten somewhere in our personal basements?

Imagine how fun it would be to play again that musical instrument you studied until you were 15 or 16 years old. And what to say about that talent you used to have to write short stories in high school, and that was never developed beyond that? Could it be that there is a creative genius incubated inside each one of us, being suffocated by the 12 hours of daily work, TV shows and other media attractions that transform us in passive observers of somebody else's creations, that not necessarily are aligned to our personal values and life priorities? Could it be that our talents as leaders, teachers, listeners, would be useful to people other than the ones in our workplace?

Unfortunately, our minds have been trained since early ages to think as "Homo Economicus," meaning, if there is no compensation or financial benefit, it is just not worth doing it. We end up with the misleading and vile perception that we are making bad use of our time. But is it really true? Wouldn't it be a much better use of your time if instead of watching TV, you would write a poem, paint a picture, create a new recipe, give private classes, learn a new language, listen to a friend or someone in need of tutoring? Shouldn't we cultivate a Da Vinci Complex in our lives, without the need to have financial compensation for every activity and for each use of our time?

I'd like to invite you to question if there is really the need for us to be such slaves of specialization and the economic utilization of every useful moment of our lives; to analyze if we are really making the best use of our free time. Wouldn't there be a dormant Da Vinci inside each one of us? Can't we break this routine spell and paint our days with a unique set of colors? What if you start developing a new talent, starting today?

And let's liberate ourselves from the obligation of being an artistic genius, a musical virtuoso, a marathon champion, or a Nobel Prize writer. The idea is to just break the vicious circle of the monochromatic specialization that makes our lives true productive monologues, denying the necessary space for us to express ourselves and put out to the world our creative abilities.

Let's make our lives more plural and colorful. Let's express what we have and carry inside of us, in multiple ways beyond our daily jobs. Seek not the Da Vinci Code, but the Da Vinci Complex.

Prisoners of the Cost-Benefit Analysis

"Anyone who stops learning is old, whether at twenty or eighty. Anyone who keeps learning stays young. The greatest thing in life is to keep your mind young."

Henry Ford

Many years ago, on a sunny Sunday afternoon, while observing my children interact with a group of friends, I couldn't help getting impressed on how easy it was for them to take decisions about playing this way or that way, to create a different way of playing, to venture themselves in a new activity and take all sorts of risks such as climbing on a tree or wall, throw things at each other, get tangled with the dog, play in the rain or get wet from head to toes as they play with water. They were experiencing a freedom unique and typical of infants and teenagers, that most of us adults have lost somewhere down the road.

As I admired and, to a degree, envied this amazing freedom of my little ones, I began to backtrack and analyze my own life story. I began to remember, and to a subtle level even relive, this wonderful sensation that we all experience when we are younger, that If there is the slightest chance of something fun to happen, we would do it and would do it immediately. Not in a while, or in a few days, or next month. We would do it right there then.

When I was little, all I needed was a friend to knock at my door or simply pass in front of my house, for me to feel a spark of excitement running up and down my body that would set me on fire. We were about to transform ourselves into invincible superheroes of fun, creativity, invention and make-believes. The only limit we would have would be the end of the afternoon, when a grumpy and boring adult (I know that my mother was nothing like that, but since she was the one to interrupt my fun time, that is how I would see her) would call us in to take a shower and have dinner. That is why I believe a shower has such a bad connotation for children. It symbolizes the apocalyptical end of their creative freedom and risky activities. It "washes away" from each of them, all the marks and signals that would serve as evidence that, even for a brief moment, they were Batman, Pelé (or Messi for today's generation), rode a motorcycle, drove a racing car, flied over the neighborhood, and saved the good-looking girl from the bad guys. After the shower, each child goes back to the limits of a clean, good smelling being, confined to the tangible and palpable realism of adults.

During my teenage years, everything was possible. Nothing had limits or barriers for someone full of hormones and unlimited energy. I still carried the soul of an infant that was then residing in a bigger and more powerful body. Such a perception of power had me mislead and made me believe I was already an adult, with answers for all questions of life.

In those days, all I needed was a glance, a sign, a phone call for the "let's do this" spirit to incorporate and, like magic, everything would happen. A party, a barbecue, ball game, traveling, roller-coaster, skip class, fool the teacher, escape from parents, steal kisses, and even those precocious "adult moments" that were so exciting then, but have us worried today, as parents. In this beautiful moment of our lives, everything can be done, nothing is tiring, nobody is too far, time is not a barrier, nothing can wait for tomorrow, everything floats around thoughts such as "I can," "I know," "I am capable," "it's going to be great," "it's going to work out." Facing your fears is most of the time a matter of having the right friend at the right time and it's done. We would win the fight together. This explosive combination of an infant soul in an almost adult body builds up the sensation of being invincible, that you can change the world, and that you can do it today!!!

Even when I was in my early twenties, I remember still carrying with me the notion that pros would always supersede the cons and that if there was even a small possibility of something to work out, I would take my chances and would try to make things happen. To go out, all I needed was a call and a good reason like, such and such people are going, this is a new place, there will be live music (we didn't even know who was singing or what kind of music would be played, but in fact, it didn't matter). If it was a weekday, the next day we would have lots of coffee and would work through the day no matter what. Romance adventures were always worth it (which evidently wasn't true, but nobody would care anyways).

The fact is that something changed down the line and I must confess that during that reflective moment, while I was observing the infantile omnipotence of that group of kids transforming everything in fun and experimentalism, I could not locate in time and space where and when this free, creative and all mighty spirit lost its way, and began to relinquish power, and most importantly, why and how it happened.

It was only after a few days, in a family discussion over some kind of plan or potential future activity, that the answers to the why and how hit me crystal clear in my mind. While the kids, with their hunger for adventure, would argue in favor of the idea or initiative, my wife and I would search for every possible argument to demonstrate to them where things could go wrong. When those discussions take place, adults will find all sorts of arguments. "It might rain," "The sun is too strong," "There will be mosquitos all over the place," "That's too far," "What if nobody else goes?," "This is going to be too expensive," and it goes on and on and on. Suddenly I had the awareness that I was on the opposite side of the conversation. The cons were now superseding the pros. I realized that I was no longer taking too many risks. I wasn't as inventive as I used to be. I would not accept the first invitation thrown at me.

I would no longer get excited about any adventure. And do you want to know why? Because, like many other adults, I had become a prisoner of the Cost-Benefit analysis.

At same point in our lives, we get introduced to this mental math, this plus and minus process that takes place inside our heads that, if well used, will spare us from many unfortunate moments, undesired situations, unnecessary expenses, and waste of energy on things that do not bring us any joy. However, as we transform this powerful decision-making tool into our permanent frame of thought, we are running the risk of taking it to the extreme, allowing it to govern. As we grant permission to the Cost-Benefit Analysis to rule our lives as the only path for decision making, we become its prisoners and that is where the danger is. As we, year after year, continuously blow the candles of our lives, the "cost" of things will only go up. We no longer have the same level of energy. That search for adventure is not around anymore. We become less and less open to changes.

Money has "cost" us so much to be earned, our time has become "more expensive," the use of our energy needs to be duly rationed and rationalized.

Stop and think for a moment on how we sometimes end up replicating this behavioral pattern in the day to day of our lives.

"Go to the mall just for an ice-cream? Oh no. Imagine the pain of driving aaaaaall the way there, finding a parking space, staying in line, and sometimes the ice cream is not even worth it."

"Go to the park to play ball now? Under this heavy sun? Are you crazy? And besides, soon it will be lunch time."

"Change this process? Why? It has served us so well until today. Why should we go through all this work without even knowing if the change is going to work?"

"Going on a trip now, at this time of the year when everything is full and more expensive? No way, I'm out. Staying home will certainly be more 'beneficial.'"

"Meet new people at this point of my life? What for? I already know so many people. And besides, the way that people are crazy nowadays, you never know what you will find."

"Have a new relationship? Not a chance. I have suffered way too much with my separations and there are no good options out there. Plus, dating at this age is ridiculous."

"Learn new things at this time of my life? And where am I going to use it?"

As we follow this line of thought, we have already fallen into the trap without realizing it. Without us noticing, the Cost-Benefit analysis already reigns sovereign. It has surrounded us like a Boa-constrictor, has us prisoners and is suffocating us little by little, taking the air out of our lungs, squeezing every breath of life we have inside.

As we scrutinize every step and decision we take in our lives through the lenses of the Cost-Benefit analysis, we begin to limit ourselves as human beings. We stop experimenting. We stop taking risks. We stop creating, innovating, daring, and reinventing ourselves. And as the years advance, and with them the "costs" involved in every decision, we stop living little by little. In other words, we begin to die.

Once I heard that either you are green and growing, or you are getting grey and dying, and that being green and growing is a state of mind, an approach, or a decision we take about our lives.

Of course, nobody will get away from getting old and dying, but we can surely delay this process by making our lives something more fun and adventurous, running some risks and making things that, every now and then, contradict the mental math that tells us that something is not worth it.

As I reached this sad conclusion that I had become a captive of the Cost-Benefit analysis, I decided to reevaluate my approach to decisions and the way I live my life. I want to keep myself green and growing for many more years, even if my hair and beard tell me a different story every time I look at myself in the mirror. What matters is what is inside. I want to keep creating, learning new things, meeting more people, having more ice cream, and playing more ball under the sun with my kids. One day, when age takes over, and it will, I will be at peace with myself, knowing that I did not allow things to precipitate before its time.

Now, what about you? How have you been using Cost-Benefit analysis in your life? Have you used this tool in a positive way or have you allowed yourself to become its prisoner? Have you adventured yourself a bit? Have you created different things lately? Have you met new people? Have you allowed yourself to live? Or have you been allowing the "cost" of things to limit, restrict or incarcerate you? Inside, are you green and growing or are you getting grey and dying?

I invite you to think about the role that the Cost-Benefit analysis has in your life and how it could limit your moments of pleasure and all sorts of growth (family, love life, social and professional). I would like to raise this awareness that, many times, without noticing, we reinforce this line of thought that limits us, and makes us old before our time.

I hope that deep inside, you are always green and growing.

BE THE MAESTRO OF YOUR LIFE

"Mastering others is strength. Mastering yourself is true power."
Lao Tzu

Have you ever taken the time to observe one of those large symphonic orchestras with dozens of professional musicians, an incredible diversity of instruments, and all varieties of sounds? It's incredible when you watch this group of musicians individually playing their own instruments, come together to make the most beautiful melodies (which were often times written centuries ago by the greatest musical geniuses of our history), emerge in an integrated and harmonic way.

These music professionals have studied their instruments for years and years and have mastered each chord that they need to bring out of them. They rehearse individually and in groups for uncountable hours until they know to perfection what to play, when to play and how to play it. When they finally get together for the presentation, they already know their music score back to front, and are more than ready to make everything come out perfectly, in a way that the audience will witness a great spectacle.

But what could be missing in this picture? The musicians are ready in their positions, their instruments have been duly tuned and the curtains have been opened. We may begin the presentation, correct? Of course not. We are missing a figure that is likely to exemplify, as few others, the meaning of the word leadership. We are missing the Maestro.

But wait a minute. If the musicians are professionals and already know each square inch of their instruments and each sound or chord they can get from them, if they have studied back to front the history of each musical genius, if they already know each line of their music scores and have rehearsed individually and collectively to exhaustion, knowing precisely what they have to play, when and how, why would they be missing a Maestro??? They all know what to do. They are masters in their instruments. So, what do they need a Maestro for??? Couldn't they just start playing and make the presentation by themselves??? It is possible that they could, but it would not be the same thing without the Maestro, and you know why? They would be missing the emotion.

It is in the hands of the Maestro the execution of one of the most important roles of a leader. To make sure that each musician of the orchestra not only reproduces with mastery what is on paper, but that they do it with the required emotion, not just any emotion, but the emotion that was present in the musical genius that wrote that play centuries ago. It is up to the Maestro to remind each musician what that melody is willing to pass to others, assuring that he/she will carry along to the audience the same energy and vibration. It is the responsibility of the Maestro that the musicians not only play the music, but that they interpret it with enthusiasm. Without this ingredient brought by his leadership, the song would be played, but it would not be the same.

You must be thinking, "Ok Marcos, I get it!!! The Maestro is important. But that has nothing to do with me. I am not an orchestra musician, even less a Maestro." And to that I ask, are you sure?

What if we go through an analogy exercise together, transferring the figure of the Maestro to our daily lives? Think of the uncountable situations when you occupy a position of leadership and you could be just waiting for the musicians to play by themselves, according to the scores.

Let's take as a first example our daily work, whatever work that may be. You are sure to be interacting with other people. Customers, suppliers, direct reports, bosses, coworkers. If we exclude the ones that have just been hired or are being trained in new functions, almost everybody knows what to do, correct? They already know their routines and have studied their disciplines. It is understandable that one would simply expect them to do their work and that they would not need anything else, right? If we think this way, we will be wasting a unique opportunity to create an impact on our work environment with positive energy and vibes. If we help these people reminding them of what is behind each task, of how the execution of their parts have an influence on the big picture, that it does make a difference to someone, on how their individual contributions will impact the future of the organization, we can certainly inspire these people and have them not only reproducing what is in the music scores, but to play a beautiful melody, with much more emotion. Especially if you have a leadership role in an organization, it is up to you to make your team (the orchestra) execute their functions (their instruments) with emotion and intensity, so the result (the music) will come out in a way that it will impress management, internal and external customers (the audience).

In our personal lives this analogy also applies to perfection. Being in the position of a father, a mother, husband, or wife, we shall never assume that the people around us simply "know what to play and how to play it." Our kids may certainly go through all the school years with good grades and end up graduating in something. However, if we don't touch them frequently and consistently with our voices of leadership showing them the relevance of their studies, building with them a vision of their future, and bringing to them a word of encouragement so they express themselves, shine and show to the world their personal talents, they are likely to play their instruments, but will not impress any audience. Our life partners may certainly spend their days by our side, but the emotion that we bring, or neglect to bring to these relationships, and the way we express or omit to express our love for these individuals, may simply make the difference between being tolerated or being a source of happiness and harmony. It is our enthusiasm as Maestros of these relationships that is certain to bring out the music that will touch the hearts of such special people.

Many other examples could be given on how we can make a difference to the world around us exercising the role of a Maestro, bringing emotion and intensity to those who are simply reproducing what is in the music score. However, I would like to call your attention to the person that might be in the highest need of your presence as a Maestro at this moment. You. Yes, you, that is reading this in this very moment. Have you ever noticed that you are actually your own Maestro, and that in this moment you could be just reproducing what is in the music scores without any emotion?

The subject being discussed here is not new and even less revolutionary, but it could go unnoticed for many reasons. We are talking about self-leadership, meaning the principle of being a leader of our own selves, pointing the way that we want to follow and putting the right level of energy, vibration, and emotion in the effort to reach our personal goals.

Many times we are distracted by the rush of our day to day, the need of leading our families, our teams at work or even taking care of our friends, our houses, paying our bills,

Flowers on the Balcony

running to the supermarket, taking care of the dog, that we end up forgetting to take care of someone unique in the universe, full of dreams and aspirations, divine light and a heart full of good things to be shown to the world. We forget to take care of ourselves, to give ourselves that extremely important and needed time to stop, look in the mirror and ask, "What about you? What do you want? What are your needs at this moment? What would you like to be doing with your life? Are you happy? How is your health? What are your dreams? What are your objectives for the next six months? And for the next three years? How do you see yourself ten years from now? And what do you need to start doing right now, to be happier? For your health to get better? For your six months, three years, and ten years objectives to materialize? How are your relationships with your kids, parents, life partners, friends, coworkers? Where the emotion of a Maestro could be missing? In which hidden corners of your life could you be just reproducing the score and the music is coming out murky and without intensity, making the audience, which in many cases is also yourself, yawn in boredom?"

If you saw yourself in any of these situations, it is time for you to change this game around. The time has come for you to take the baton, knock it on the wood getting the attention of the orchestra that, before I forget, is your own self, and start playing the many instruments that make the music of your life sound with more emotion and intensity, since between you and me, if you don't do it, nobody else will. Or even worse, someone else could be taking the baton and orchestrating the music of your life in your place. In this very moment you could be playing music that is not yours, in somebody else's orchestra, being led to directions you did not choose. In this very second someone else could be orchestrating what you want or need in matters such as your health, your happiness, your dreams, your objectives. So, it's time to ask, could it be that the music you are playing in this or that aspect of your life is murky and without emotion because it is not your music, but the music that someone else is orchestrating in your life? Or could it be that you have abandoned the baton and left yourself alone, without your own leadership, without your own energy and vibration, and started playing your music without enthusiasm, just looking at the paper and reproducing note by note?

Let's then close our analogy by thinking of the moment that you, as the Maestro of your life, will turn the last page of the score to make the orchestra play the final notes, the last chord, and go "taraaaaammmm!!!" . . . What would be the reaction of the audience? Would they be on their feet applauding enthusiastically? Will they ask for an encore? Or would it be that the audience is reduced to half a dozen spectators that just tolerated the presentation until the end, will politely applaud for a few seconds, and leave the theater in relief?

As you position yourself as the leader of your own life, or as the Maestro of your own orchestra, how do you visualize the last act? Is the exhibition moving towards a melancholic end or towards a "Grand Finale"? If the answer to this question was not the one you would like, there is still time. The show is not over yet. It is still possible to take over the baton and make the orchestra of your life play the most beautiful and enthusiastic melodies, either at home, at work, or in the relationships with people that really matter to you.

Just remember this. As you take over the baton, you are the Maestro. Make a difference. Be the leader of your own life. Be your own Maestro and make your own music come out so beautiful, that it will be impossible not to amaze the most diverse audiences, including yourself.

LIVING LIFE TO THE FULLEST AS IF WE WERE GOING TO DIE

"All we have to decide is what to do with the time that is given to us."
Gandalf in "Lord of the Rings; The Fellowship of the Ring"

We all have heard a tale like this before, many, many times. Everything is going well in the life of a person, his/her work is following its routine, the family is coming along fine on their day to day, friendships are following their course, when suddenly . . .Bang!!! Something happens and that person goes through a near death experience. An accident, a heart attack, an airplane that almost falls, and unexpectedly, this person sees herself face to face with the possibility of death.

The innumerous descriptions of experiences of this kind have a lot in common. The majority of the people involved say that they mentally revised all their lives in just a few seconds, and that after they went through and survived such a situation, they started looking at their existence from a different angle. As an example, we could mention that some reevaluated their relationships, reaching the conclusion that some were actually not positive for them and not worth keeping. Others thought over their professional lives and understood that they were tolerating jobs and situations that were not contributing in anything to them. And there were even those who felt selfish with the less fortunate ones, realizing they had done little charity work during their lives. But what we most commonly hear from these people is that they thought about their relationships with the ones they loved the most. Many spoke about feeling desperation when they realized they most likely wouldn't be able to hug their wives/husbands and kids one last time, that they wouldn't be able to say "I love you" to parents that are far away, to a friend or relative that was very dear to them, or even to say "thank you" to people that contributed relevantly during their existence.

Famous best-selling writer and Executive Coach Marshall Goldsmith describes a moment of desperation like this in his book *What Got You Here Won't Get You There*. He tells that in one of his many business trips, the plane he was traveling had some serious technical problems and needed to land without the landing gear, giving every indication that the flight could come to a tragic end. During those endless moments of panic, Marshall thought about his life, his exaggerated devotion to work, and the limited time he used to spend with his wife and kids. But the most reveling thought was that he felt he had been ungrateful to many people. He realized that his success was the result of positive influences of individuals like his parents, some teachers, mentors, coworkers, and friends that he had never taken the time to thank appropriately for being such difference makers, enabling him to get as far as he did in life.

Fortunately, the tragic end never happened. That day, after escaping alive from such a difficult experience, Marshall took the decision to change all that. From that moment on he started seeking a greater balance between his personal and professional lives and began to take even better care of his health. But the most interesting new resolution was that he was going to put an end to his self-proclaimed ingratitude. Marshall made some Certificates of Relevant Contribution (or something of the like) with a Thank You message and sent them to the people he understood had contributed in a decisive manner for him to be the successful person he is. And beyond that gesture, he decided to make the habit of saying "Thank You" almost like a religion, always sincerely recognizing any contribution or action, no matter how small, with these two magic words.

So now I ask, why do so many people have to get to this type of extreme experience of a close encounter with death to reevaluate their lives and change them in such profound ways? Why do we cultivate the deceptive notion that we will live forever, or that we will all die at the age of 95 and will have plenty of time to correct all our wrong doings, fix all our relationships, say "I love you" or "I am sorry, and I apologize" to everyone we haven't said it until today? How many stories of early death do we know where these poor souls did not have the second chance that Marshall had? What guarantees do we have that we will live yet for many years, and that time is on our side so that "one day" we may swallow our prides and say "I am sorry, please forgive me" to someone we hurt before? What guaranties do we have that we will come back from work or from the gym today? There is a Brazilian pop song that says, "We need to love as if there is no tomorrow, because if you stop to think of it, in fact, there isn't."

Another example of self-transformation that is worth mentioning is the story of Randy Pausch. Randy was a professor at Carnegie Mellon, one of the best universities in the US, with a brilliant future ahead of him, happy in his marriage and father of three beautiful little children. At the peak of his career, Randy was diagnosed with irreversible pancreatic cancer and was informed that he had only a few months to live. Randy's first reaction was the same as any human being. He was full of self-pity, could not believe what was happening to him and kept asking the "why me" question. He was also desperate about what could happen to his wife and kids after he was gone. After that, he began to feel miserable and depressed. However, at a given point he concluded that feeling miserable and depressed would not bring his health back and would help the future of his family even less, so he decided he would continue to work and would write and record messages to his kids, so they could see and hear them when they grow up. Randy's work was soon noticed by friends. With the help of some people, his writings and messages became a book called The Last Lecture that came to be a best seller and helped build a financial safety net for his family, that before, simply wasn't there. It is a habit of some American universities to have a professor to offer what has been named The Last Lecture. The professor pretends this to be his last message and talks about things that really matter or people that inspired him/her. Well, in Randy's case his Last Lecture was indeed the last one and took place in a packed auditorium on September 18th, 2007. It was recorded on video and it's still very popular on YouTube searches today. Whoever watches Randy's energy and vibe during his lecture would never guess that he was under the effect of chemotherapy and living his last months. Randy died on July 27th, 2008, at the age of 47, leaving behind a legacy to his kids and to humanity with his book, his video, his example of life and way of dying. He lived the last days of his life literally as if he was dying. Because he was.

Flowers on the Balcony

As we look at these two examples and maybe many others you might know, I believe the strongest message that comes to mind is that we shall live life like there is no tomorrow. We shall live as if every second really matters and as if every interaction we have with the ones we love would be the last one. We shall live like we are dying.

Once I read that the odds you would wish you had spent more time at the office when you are in your deathbed are very little, and that who will most likely be there to support you in this final transition will not be your former bosses and coworkers, but the ones who really love and care about you. And isn't that so true? As we picture this scene in our heads, the regrets that cross our minds are the moments we missed having with our families or friends, the words of affection we did not say, the caress we did not give. We ask ourselves if we did something really relevant with the time that was given to us in this existence. Futilities and secondary things such as the extra few pounds we carry or the arguable imperfections of our bodies, the type of car we drive or brand of clothes we wear, all this will certainly not come to our minds on our deathbeds. After all, we are not really living this life for these things, are we? What will really count in this moment is how much love we gave and received, how we contributed positively for the people that matter the most to us, and what we did during our lives to make this world a better place than it was, when we first came into it. We would like, as we close our eyes, to have a gratifying feeling that we lived our lives to the fullest.

So, in order to bring our reflections to a close, we need to talk about living life to the fullest and what it really means to each of us. Certainly, the answer to what living life to the fullest means will depend on each individual. Some may say it is living in harmony with the universe, whatever that means. Others may say that what really matters to them is to embrace a cause that is bigger than them, like changing a political regime of a country, save the whales, go out and preach a religion, go to Africa take care of the famine, or dedicate their lives to charity and social work.

Others may simply dream of a successful career, pile up material assets and reach the top of their profession. Independently of how you answer this question, what really matters is that the answer is genuinely yours, not borrowed or inherited from somebody else. This may sound simple, but in reality, it will require some deep reflection, since what is really important to us, many times could be covered by the mist of social conventions, someone else's values, external priorities.

In order to genuinely find your answer to this question, put yourself mentally in the position we just described. Close your eyes and imagine yourself on your deathbed. You have only a few hours ahead of you. As you think about your brief existence on this planet, what comes to your mind as things you didn't do and would like to have done? Or even things that you did, and could have or should have done more? What things or activities occupied an exaggerated portion of your time and attention, and that now present themselves clearly as secondary or as distractions that pushed you away from the things and activities that really matter? Who didn't you kiss enough, didn't hug enough, didn't say "I love you" enough? Who has contributed to your success, and you would like to say "thank you" but never took the time and attention to do it? To whom do you own an apology, but have never been humble enough to do it? What relationships have you tolerated and feel now that you shouldn't have or even didn't need to have tolerated? What dreams did you carefully nurture in your intimacy, but always waited for the perfect "alignment of planets" to live them? What changes would you like to have made in your life that you never had the courage to make, but now that you are dying, you regret the fact that you never dared?

Once you have done this exercise and answered these questions, open your eyes, and take a good look around you. Be fully aware that you are alive and very much alive, full of energy, and that there is still time. How much time? Nobody knows, and in fact it doesn't matter. What matters is that you still can do all this. You still can say "I love you," "Thank you very much," apologize and make peace, rebuild the important relationships, and eliminate the bad ones, try to make your dreams come true and finally, change, and transform your life.

As you open your eyes and feel that the pulse is still pulsing, and that life is still running through your veins, imagine that the next page of your life is a blank page yet to be written, and that the pen is in your hands. What are you going to write? But remember. The next page can always be the last one, so write it well. Write the most beautiful pages as if this was the last chapter and live like you were dying. Because you are. It's a matter of time.

Go for it. Write the rest of your story living your life to the fullest. Starting now.

Go . . .

THE TWENTY CALLS TO ACTION

"Vision without action is merely a dream. Action without vision just passes the time. Vision with action can change the world."
Joel Arthur Barker

01 - Put your flowers on the balcony and make life flourish around you.

02 - Humanize your relationships; make them something more valuable and most importantly, be the best parent your kids could possibly have.

03 - Make a difference in someone's life. Change the tangible world for the better.

04 - Expect the unexpected, and when it comes, and your life changes rhythm, sing and dance to the new music.

05 - Remember that love is what you do, therefore refine, and improve your love propositions.

06 - Avoid the extremes and seek balance; seek the middle way.

07 - Do good things to others, simply because the alternative to it is bad, and does not suit you.

08—Cultivate your mental garden, watch for the seeds you nurture, and what you allow to get in it.

09 - Forgive others and yourself.

10 - Do your best to reach your goals but leave the door open for destiny to surprise you.

11 - Seek for personal continuous improvement and win the race against your own self.

12 - Make your midlife crises become an opportunity to renovate and reinvent yourself.

13 - Have passion for what you do and create, and for the things you have, but be detached from it all, since everything passes and the new always comes.

14 - Persist, do not give up, and persevere until you shine, but let others shine as well.

15 - Manage and accept the differences you have with others, especially the ones with your loving partner.

16 - Interrupt the chain reactions of bad vibes and energy. Do not pass along the garbage of others.

17 - Wake-up the sleeping Da Vinci inside of you and create, learn something new, renovate, innovate. Do things other than your daily job.

18 - Be always green and growing, reinventing, and adventuring yourself.

19 - Be your own Maestro and make your life play the most beautiful melodies.

20 - Live your life to the fullest as if you were dying.

About the Author

Marcos H. N. Rossi is a writer, works as a Life-Coach, and teaches executive courses. He holds a Bachelor's degree in Economics and a postgraduate degree in Strategic Business Management from Unicamp. He graduated in Coaching from CoachU in the USA. He began writing in 2011, and is also the author of the books "A Mais Bela Travessia" and "Os Caminhos do Amor em Bread & Joy," both released by Underline Publishing. He lives in Florida with his wife and two children.

Made in United States
Cleveland, OH
23 October 2025